THE SCHMETTERSCHWANZ MANUSCRIPT

ALPHADESIGNER

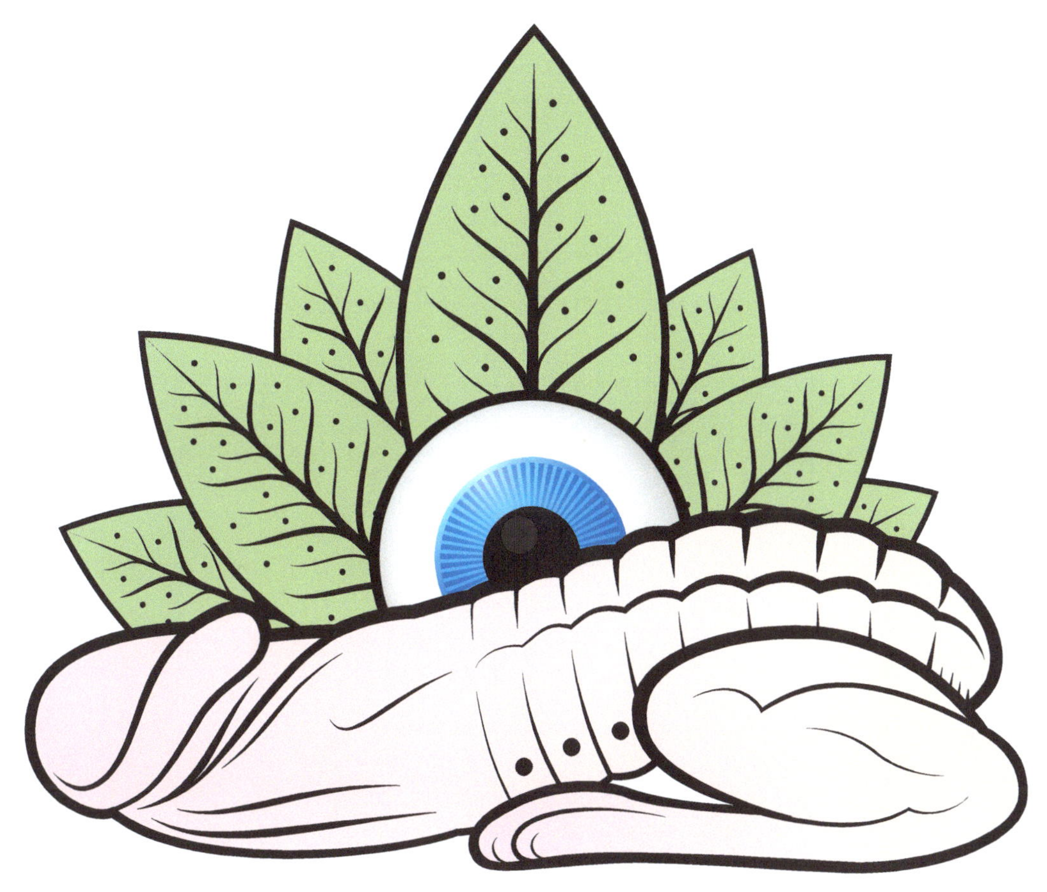

THE

SCHMETTERSCHWANZ

MANUSCRIPT

VALENCIA 2021

APOPHENIA SERIES

THE SCHMETTERSCHWANZ MANUSCRIPT

Very first edition

Created, written, and illustrated by Alphadesigner
with contributions by Yanko Tsvetkov

Design and print layout by Yanko Tsvetkov
Copy editing and typesetting by The Illuminati
Art direction by The Powers That Be
Special agent: Martin Brinkmann

Published on October 8, 2021
in Valencia (Spain) by Alphadesigner

ISBN (paperback): 978-84-09-33883-2

Official website: alphadesigner.com
Facebook: facebook.com/alphadesigner
Instagram: alphadesigner
Twitter: @alphadesigner
Email: alphadesigner@gmail.com

ISNI: 0000 0004 0208 7779
VIAF ID: 296971239

To Luigi Serafini,
who blew my fucking mind.

Foreword

The axiom *There is nothing new under the sun!* is often attributed to Pensius, a philosopher who preferred to mingle with dogs instead of people. When he died unexpectedly at the age of ninety-nine, his pets ate most of his writings except a handful of wrinkled pages, scattered all over his nightstand. They were found by his maid, Maphalda. A simple woman, she was nevertheless aware of the status of her employer, and—to spare him the reputation of being remembered as messy and chaotic, she threw them away.

Because of these unfortunate circumstances, there is no way to confirm without a reasonable doubt whether it was indeed Pensius who formulated the axiom. Nevertheless, its veracity remained unchallenged even after the *Age of Discovery*, when Saint Brendan of Compostela fell through a hole in the Sunset Ocean and discovered the Underworld—a previously unknown region of our planet unspoiled by sunlight, and therefore, extremely rich in things that are unquestionably new.

The unsolicited honor of finding something new in broad daylight fell to the lumberjack Jörg Holzhacker, a native of Schmetterdorf, a small village in the barbaric North. While cutting a rotten oak tree, this illiterate peasant stumbled upon an ancient manuscript filled with mysterious writings and imagery. Unaware of its immense value, he sold it to a fortune teller named Mesmeralda Yagishna, who used it as an inspiration for her infamous divination deck. When Mesmeralda brought the manuscript to Abharazarhadarad, it attracted the attention of natural philosopher Morpheus Baudrillard, who, mesmerized by its undecipherable symbols, immediately bought it for an undisclosed amount of gold—a reckless act that cost him his senior position in the *Council of Commercial Strategists*. The manuscript remained locked in Baudrillard's cabinet of curiosities until his death. Eager to restore their family's standing in Abharazarhadaradian society, his daughters Lana and Lilly sold it to a travelling art dealer, who eventually brought it to our kingdom, where it was confiscated under the *Protection of Literary Heritage Act*.

An urgent restoration process, led by our most distinguished conservator, Alphadesigner, began immediately after the manuscript was catalogued in our library. The parchment was straightened and scrubbed of impurities, and its content was meticulously copied on high quality paper. The primitive imagery was reinterpreted in modern style to conform to our advanced understanding of beauty and harmony. The color palette, originally limited to washed-out, earthy tones that inspire melancholy and sluggishness in the reader, was expanded with the noblest shades of green, blue, and lilac.

After the restoration was complete, the original material was recycled safely according to our highest environmental standards. The perfected copies were entrusted to our talented team of cryptographers. To our great surprise, a decade of intense cryptanalysis revealed the language was a nonsensical corruption of our own, while the letters of the arcane script were equivalent to those in our alphabet. This unexpected result prompted speculations the manuscript was an elaborate hoax. A delegation of forensic semioticians was swiftly dispatched to Schmetterdorf. Upon arrival, they found the village completely destroyed. A barbarian horde called *The Sons of Occam* had killed the entire population, except the priest, who remained hidden in the cellar of the temple. Attempts to find the tree from which Jörg Holzhacker extracted the manuscript have so far failed.

Despite the great confusion, or perhaps because of it, public interest in the manuscript is growing exponentially. To satisfy the curiosity of our readers, the *Regulatory Council of Public Entertainment* authorized the publication of a mass market edition, tailored to the needs of common readers. Once again, the task of adapting the content fell to Alphadesigner, whose dedication to the preservation of our cultural heritage rivals only that of our pragmatic Heavenly Father, Clearchus.

It is my sincere hope that future generations will succeed in demystifying this manuscript, whatever the cost might be.

Prof. Sigismund Alegrius
Chief Examiner

Library of Superb Enlightenment
Kingdom of the Word

Introduction

In the rich and eventful history of our most revered and cherished *Library of Superb Enlightenment,* there have been many books that have challenged our understanding of practicality and purpose. Among the few infamous examples are *The Knowledge Singularity*—a tell-all pseudo biography of a renegade librarian, and the overly long treatise *The Delights of Procrastination,* whose final paragraph extends over three hundred and ninety-five pages and, rather indecently, is deprived of a full stop.

These shameless attempts to scandalize our pragmatic minds have failed to leave a mark on our cultural landscape because they were obvious hoaxes, created to amuse rather than educate us.

It was in this context that I began work on *The Schmetterschwanz Manuscript*—a piece of deteriorated parchment that abounds with chaotic musings of a barbarian artist whose intellect had just awakened from its primitive slumber. Beneath the orgy of incoherent symbolism that immediately arrests the unsuspecting eye was a sincere attempt for the appreciation of complexity that we often take for granted. The value of this manuscript is not in its actual content but in what it offers us—a unique chance to observe that mysterious, unexplored state in the development of the human mind when the sense of wonder gives way to the sense of practicality.

Alphadesigner
Chief Conservator

Ministry of Aesthetic Affairs
Kingdom of the Word

On the Writing System

A civilization's writing system says a lot about its level of development and—according to some theories of evolutionary graphology—can even influence its destiny. Primitive writing is by definition simple and economical; there is neither time nor desire for aesthetic permutations, not to mention legibility concerns that would naturally occupy a contemporary typesetter's mind. It is not immediately obvious why this simplicity is unsustainable in the long run, but it is an undeniable fact that as civilizations advance, their writing becomes more complex.

As Professor W.H. Scrivener notes in his *Historia alphabetica*, an alphabet is much more than a tool that enables the storage and transmission of information. Once written down, a text becomes a standalone entity and acquires its own characteristics, independent from the content it stores or the purpose it serves. This is where aesthetics comes into play. It enables what Scrivener calls *subinfomratic metadata*, in other words, bits of subtle extra information that can, among other things, convey the authority of a source or the urgency of a message.

There is, of course, a threshold after which complexity becomes detrimental. When a text draws too much attention to its own appearance, it can easily distract the readers and even hinder their comprehension. A civilization that can find and, most importantly, maintain the right balance between informational practicality and aesthetic presentation stands at the top of the bell curve in Scrivener's *Graph of Rise and Demise of Literate Societies*. Those that indulge in extravagant aesthetics sooner or later suffer informational breakdown and societal collapse.

It was initially assumed that the script present in *The Schmetterschwanz Manuscript* was deliberately complicated as to intentionally obscure its meaning. This turned out not to be the case. It quickly became evident that the complex symbols are simply alternatives to the letters of our alphabet—a fact so unnerving, it gave rise to yet another avalanche of questions concerning the manuscript's origin and purpose. Only the future can tell whether we will find appropriate answers.

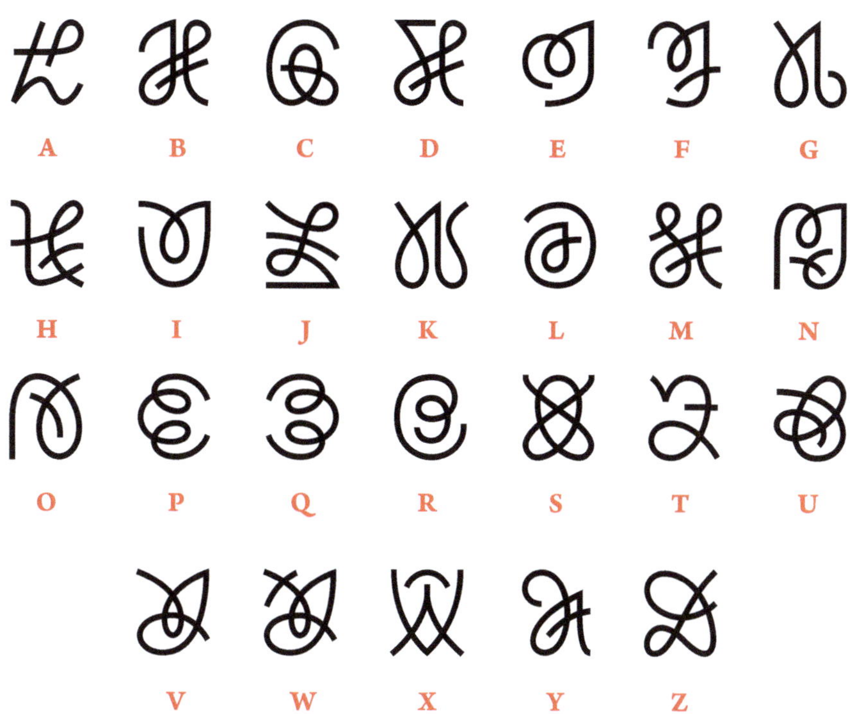

A
B
C
D
E
F
G
H
I
J
K
L
M
N
O
P
Q
R
S
T
U
V
W
X
Y
Z

Part One: Emergence

For all its flamboyant eccentricity, *The Schmetterschwanz Manuscript* opens with a depiction of a common insect, *Lytta caudilliana*. It is colloquially knows as *Caudillian fly*. A native of the North and the eastern shores of the Sunset Ocean, this blistering beetle secretes a chemical known as *catharsidin*. It is widely believed, especially in cultures where the flow of information is poorly regulated and there is no central authority to counter frivolous claims, that this chemical is an aphrodisiac. While there are no hard facts to support such an assertion, it has been positively determined that catharsidin is an extremely potent psychotropic drug that can cause intense hallucinations, emotional disassociation, detachment from reality, and—if employed on a mass scale—societal collapse.

Naturally, people who use this substance have a poorly developed sense of social responsibility. A well-documented survey among the crews of merchant ships visiting Abharazarhadarad in the span of five years established that ninety percent of the sailors used the drug at least once a week when in harbor.

With all this in mind, a team of postgraduate researchers under the supervision of Professor Severus Fulvius from the *Department of Artistic Interpretation* theorized that the true author of the manuscript must be an intoxicated sailor. To further support their claims, the researchers add that, apart from notorious consumers of aphrodisiacs, sailors are prone to wild exaggerations—a phenomenon also noticed among nomadic populations all over the world that might arise from their inability to permanently settle.

This is, of course, as far as such a theory can go, given the fact that the brief depictions of the Caudillan fly and its larvae are immediately followed by content of unclassifiable nature. Both the visuals and the supplied captions are undecipherable. The explanatory text on the third folio, for example, says:

Four-dimensional evolution of the chemical bonds inside a hive mind through progressive dismantling of a peripheral corporate ladder.

Notwithstanding the intentionally nonsensical language, the stacking of scientific and economic terms is by no means random. While no meaning can be derived from the convoluted word order, the syntax of the sentence is fairly standard and its grammar—uncorrupted.

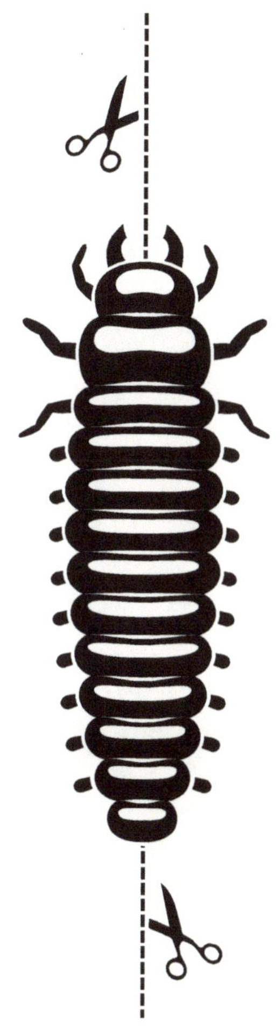

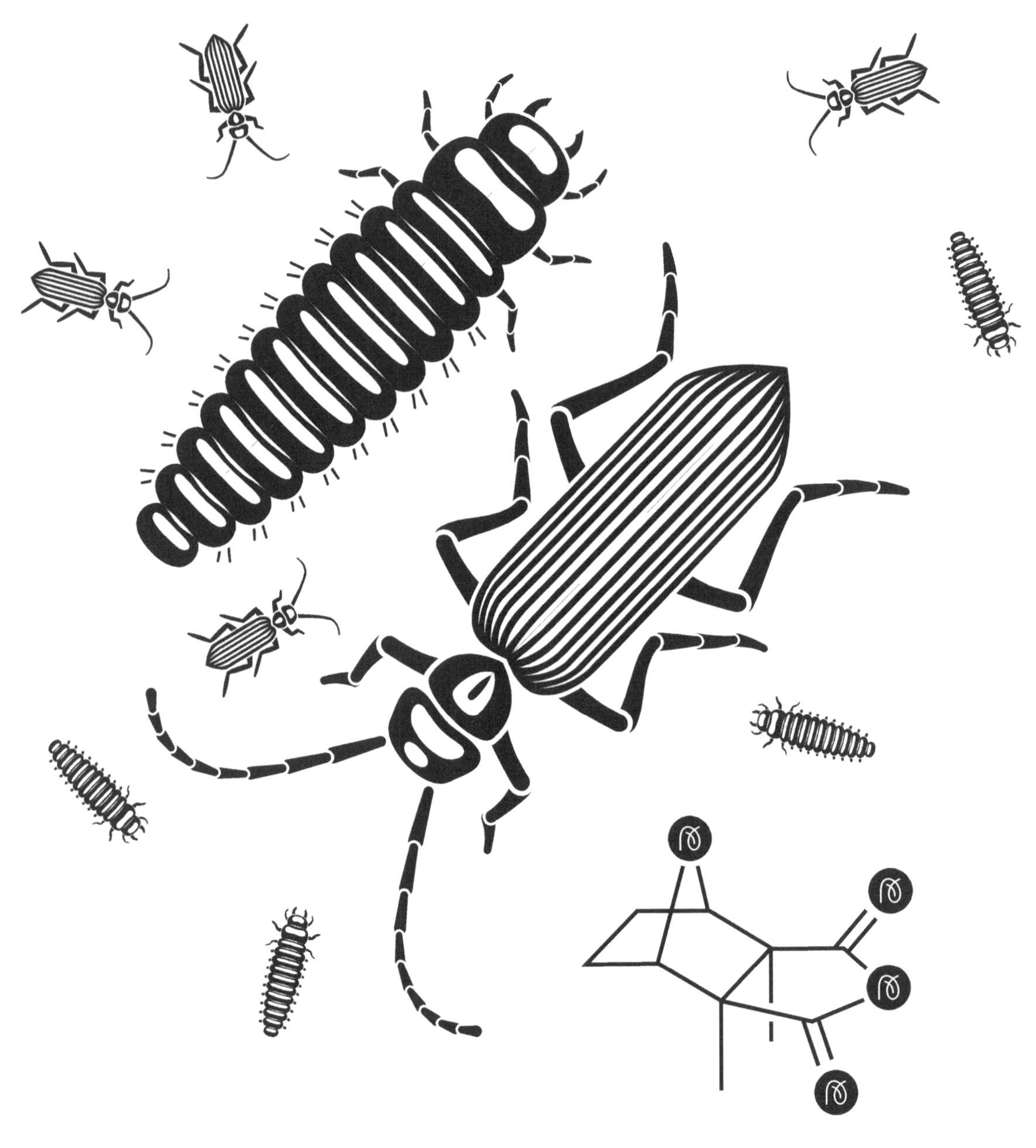

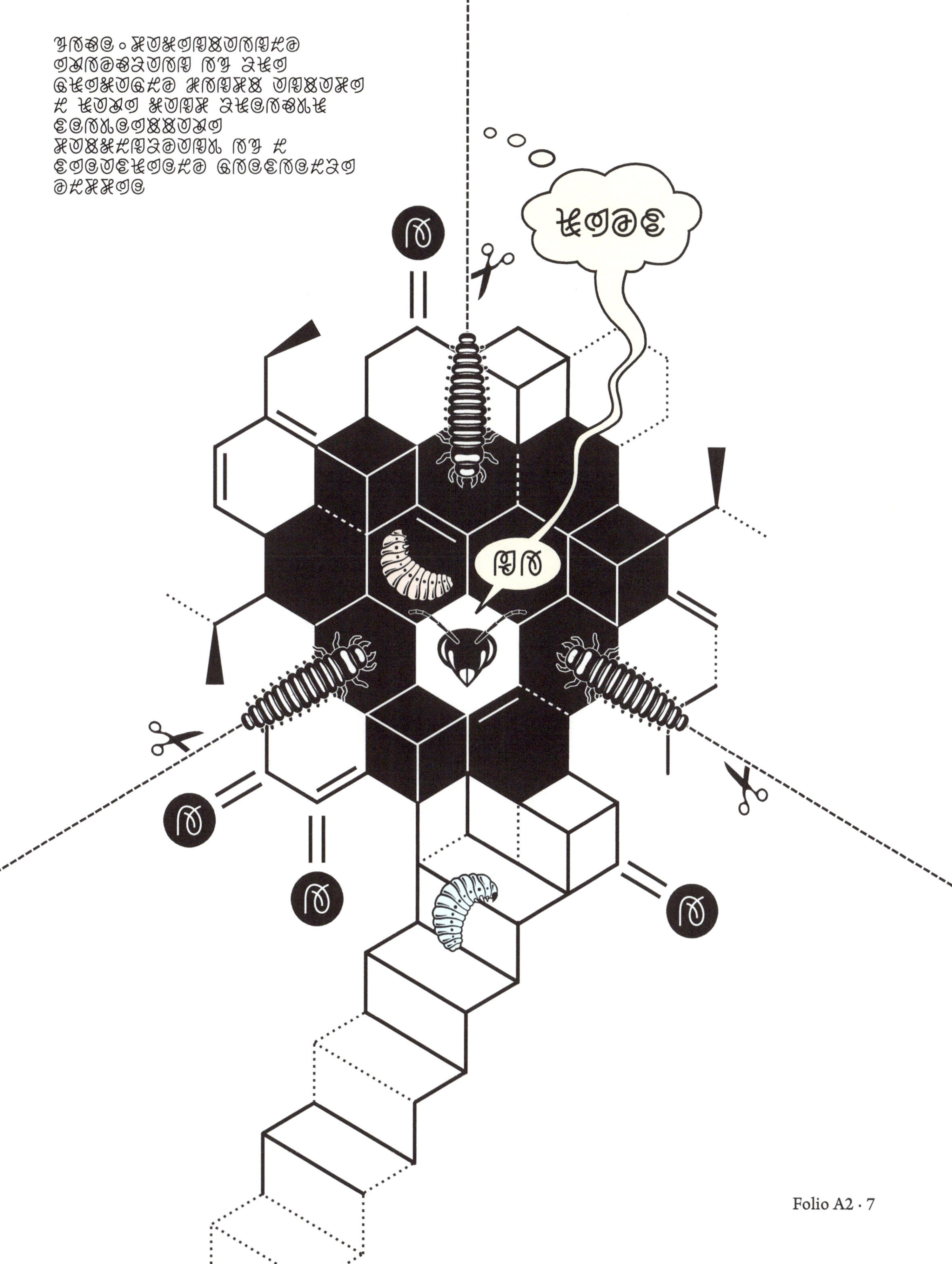

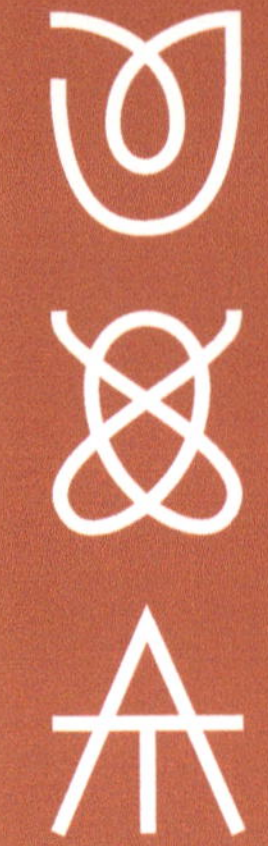

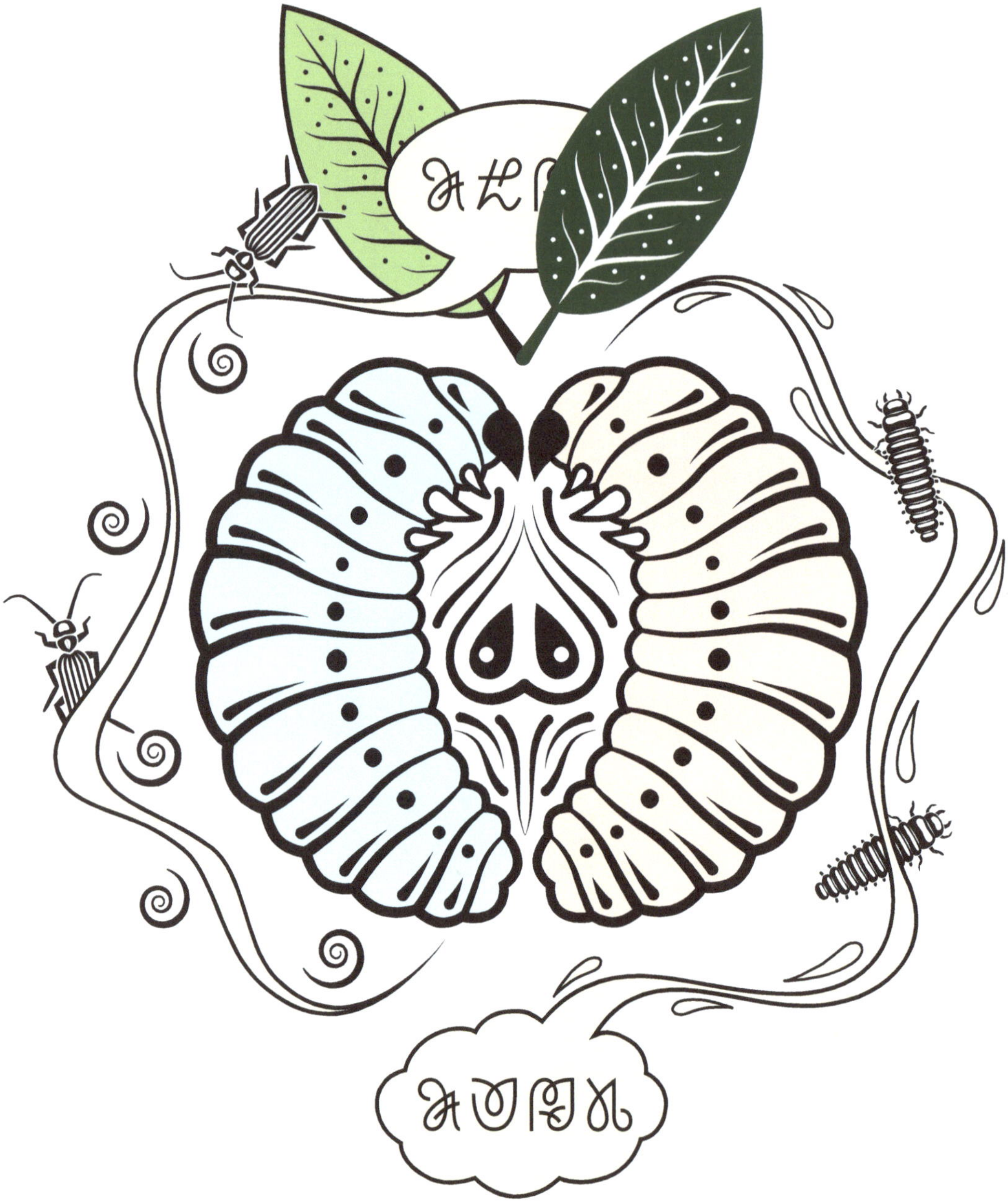

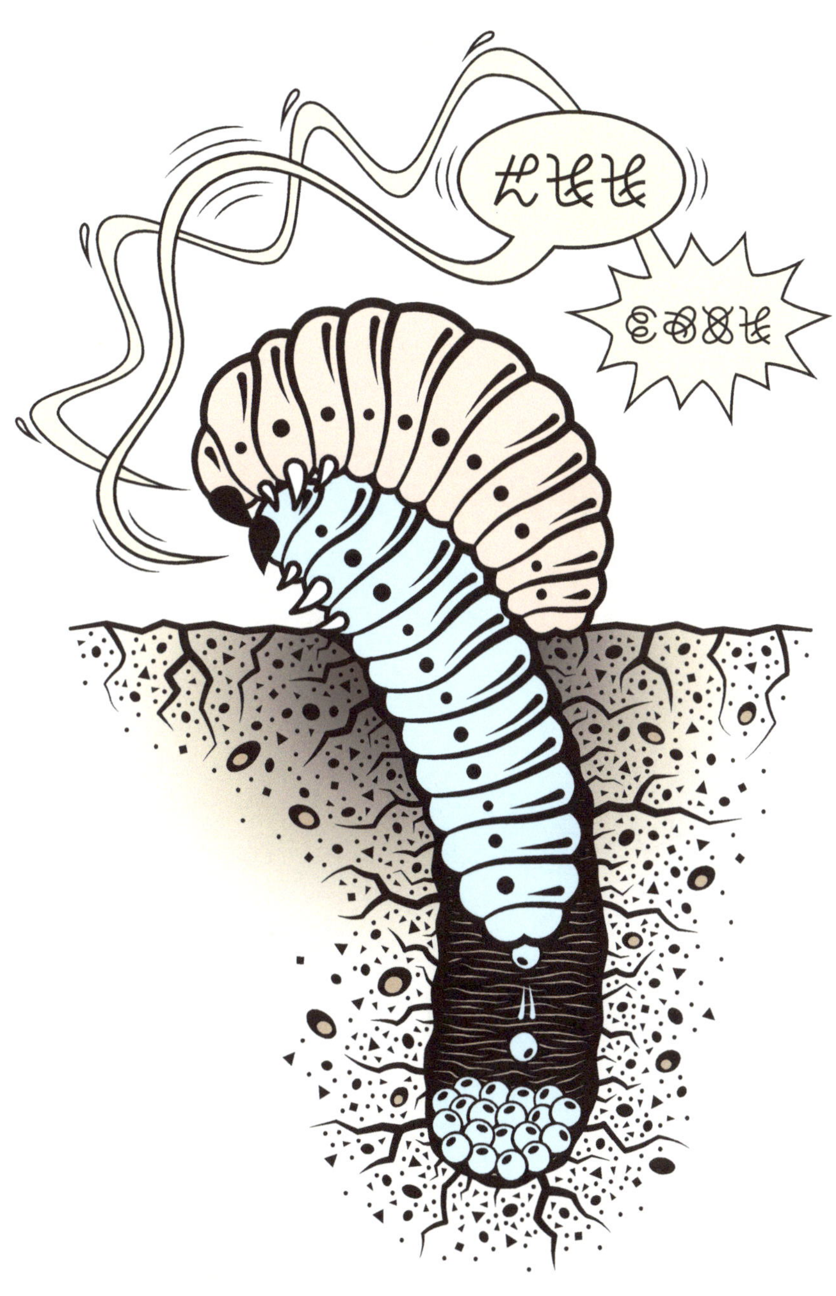

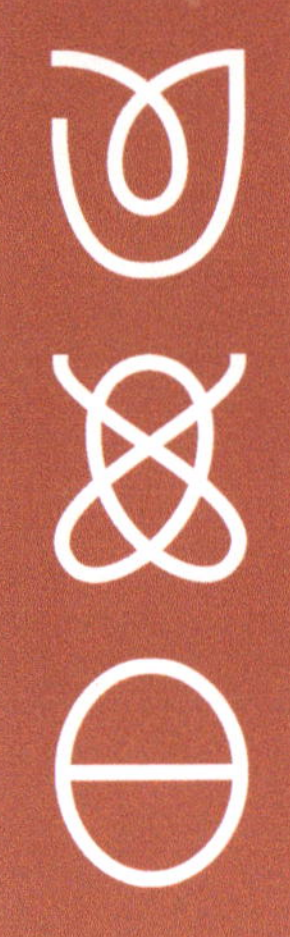

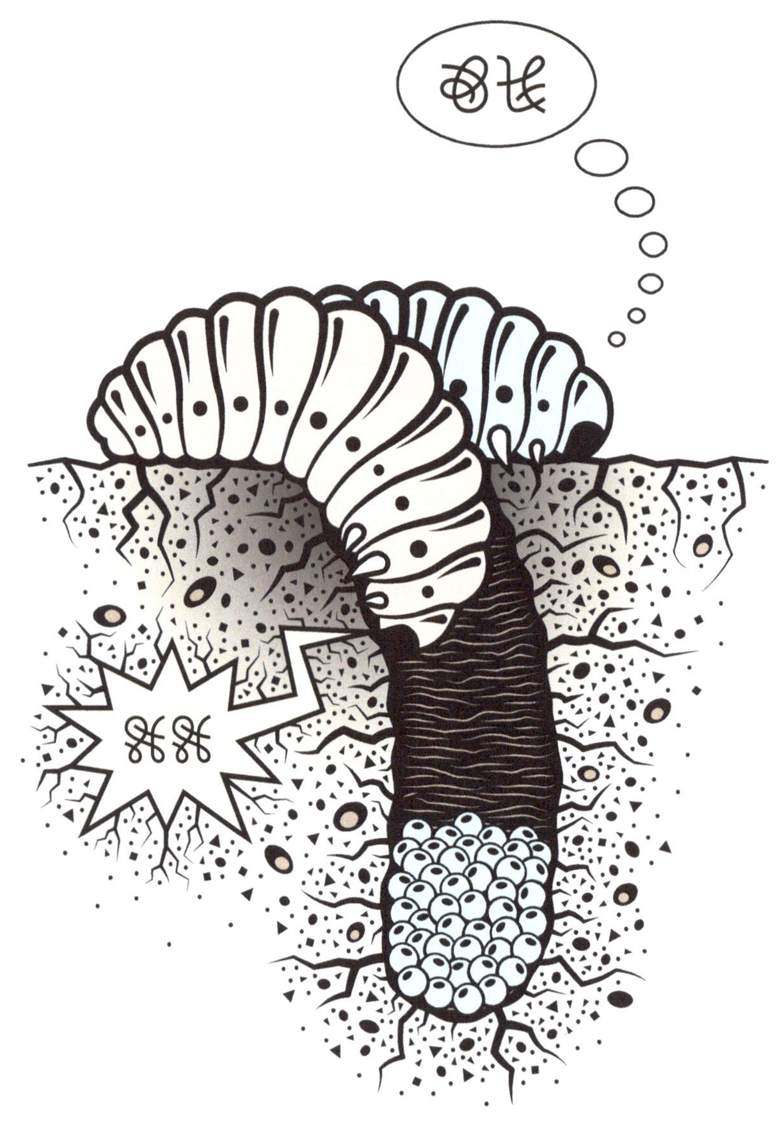

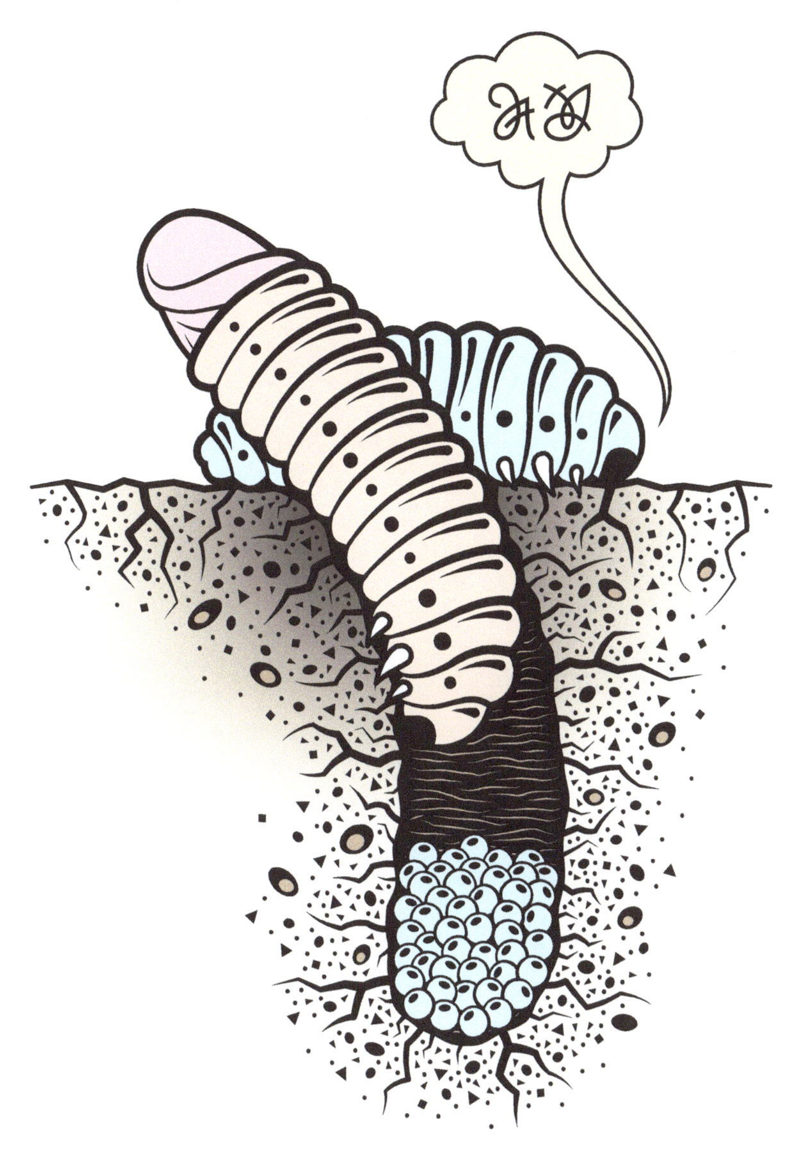

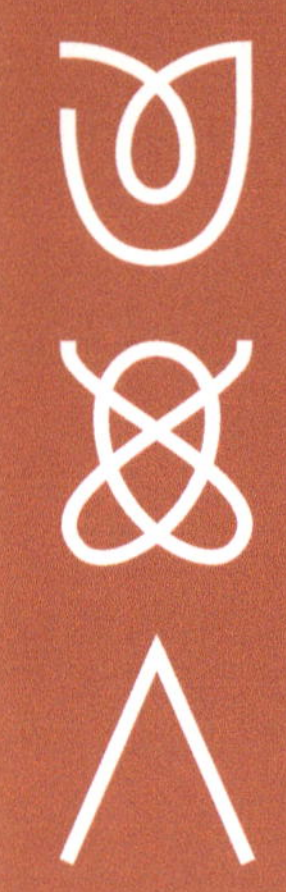

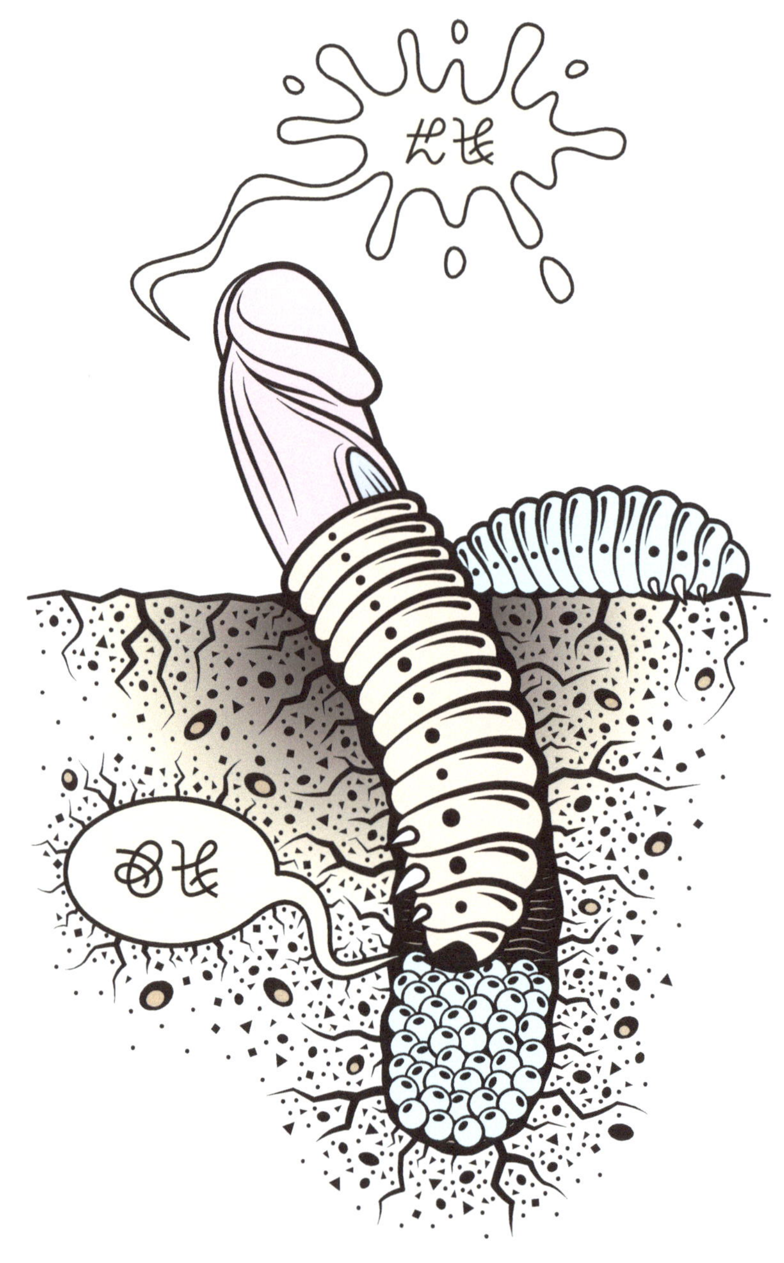

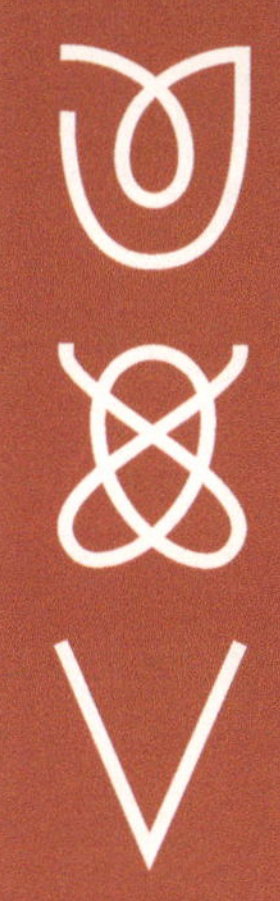

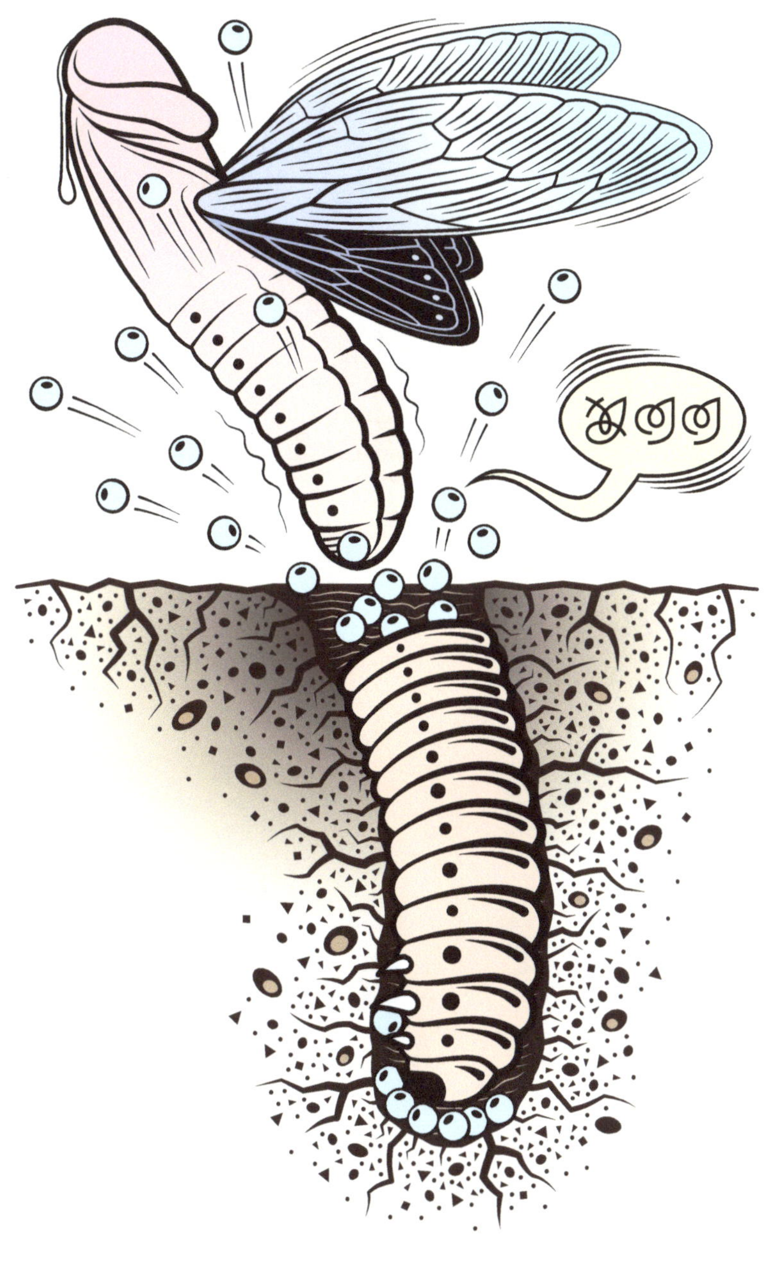

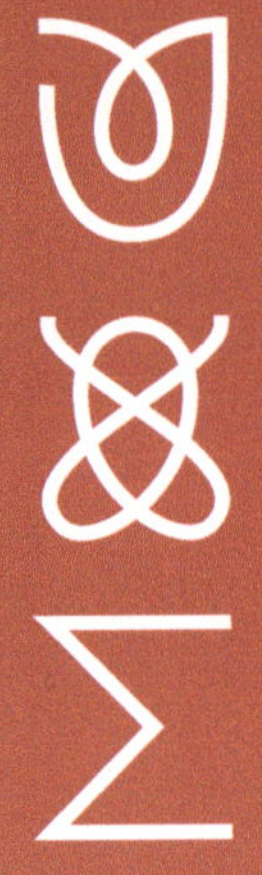

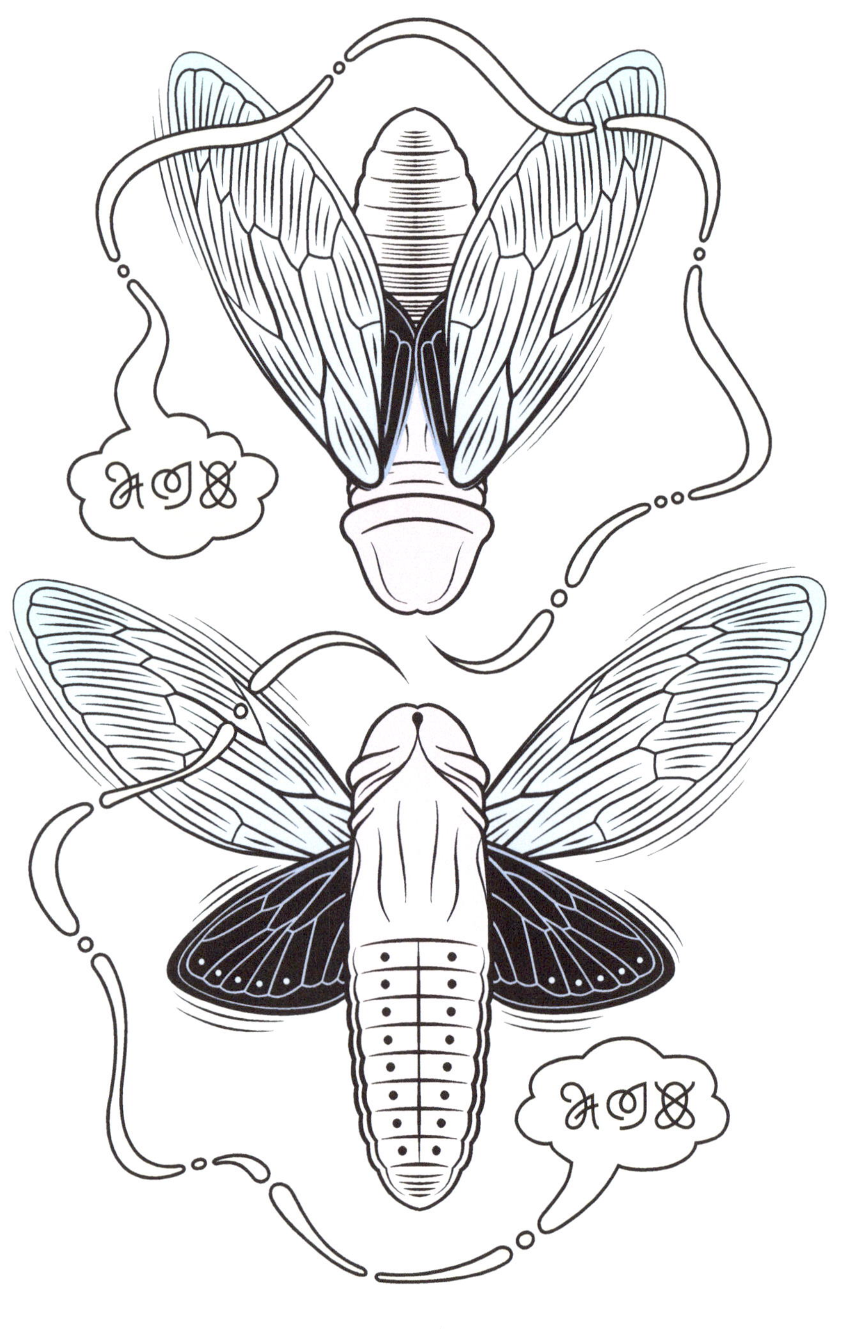

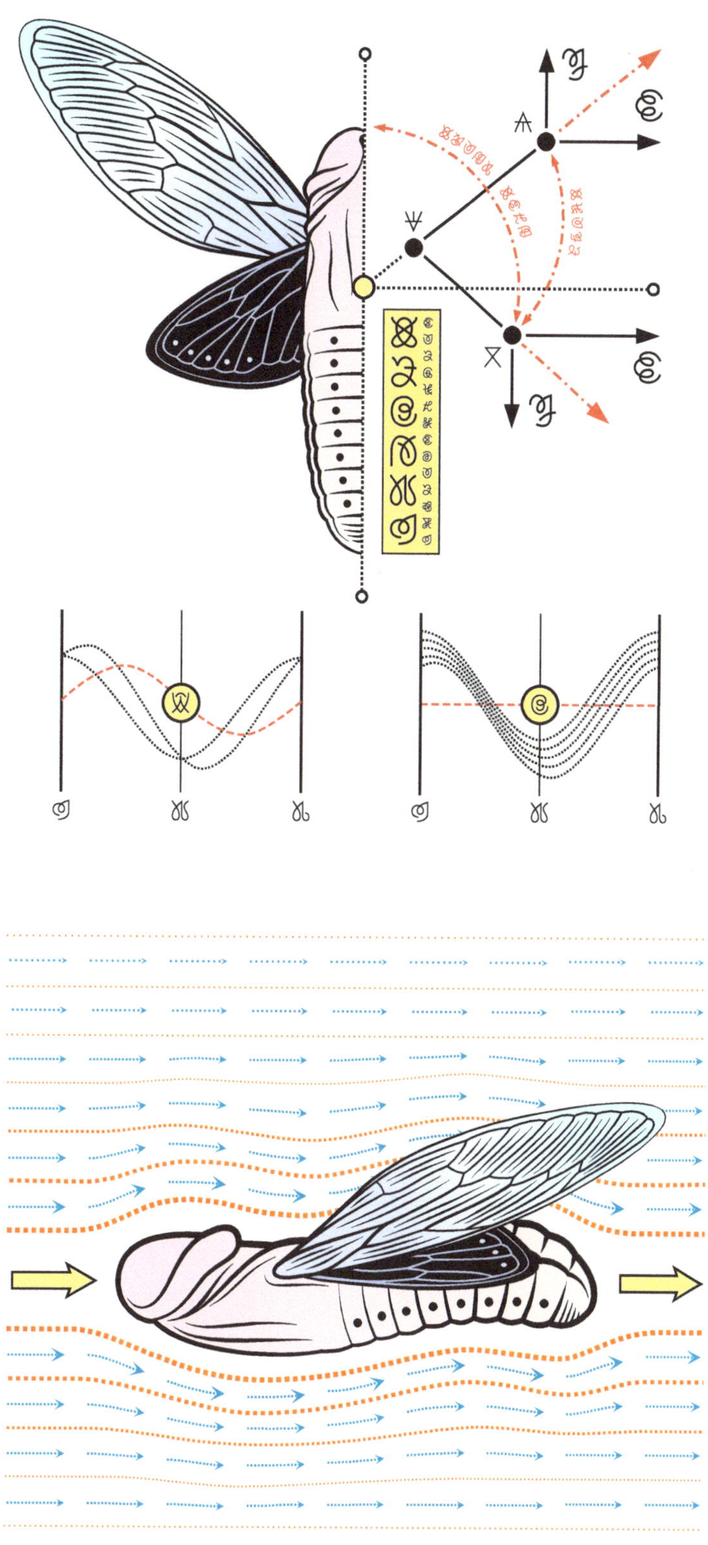

Part Two: Convergence

Even the most sophisticated of studies have humble beginnings. Philosophy can trace its origin in simple questions that have no practical value but appear instinctively amusing for undisciplined human minds. The most popular one is of course the *What came first..?* type, its most common interpretation concerning a choice between an egg and a bird.

If *The Schmetterschwanz Manuscript* is to be trusted, this premise is inherently misconceived. Eggs, it appears, come not from chicken but from airborne migratory larvae. In general, thoughtless depictions of interspecies hybrids are not unknown in anthropology. They belong to a tradition that many hunter-gatherers indulge in, especially when confronted with the limits of their natural knowledge. Reports of exotic lands like *Cynocephalia*, a kingdom inhabited by dog-headed people, abound even in the literature of advanced cultures, where they serve as entertainment.

Regardless of the context, there are no records of hybrids between incompatible biological classes. One could only guess what inspired the author to blend features of insects and avians in one single abomination, since the only common thing among them is their ability to fly. The misunderstandings are by no means related only to appearance. The first five folios depict migratory paths, and even though there is no indication of scale, the projected distances seem vast and include big spaces of open water—a challenge few insects would endure, much less on a seasonal basis.

The biological study is spontaneously interrupted by socio-economic data and hints at potential implications on the hybrid's procreation:

Macroeconomic oscillation between industrial output and consumer demand proportional to purchasing power of high-income nuclear families.

Just like in part one, the language borders on parody, which might offer some clues about the not so noble origins of "the most enlightened daughter of humor."

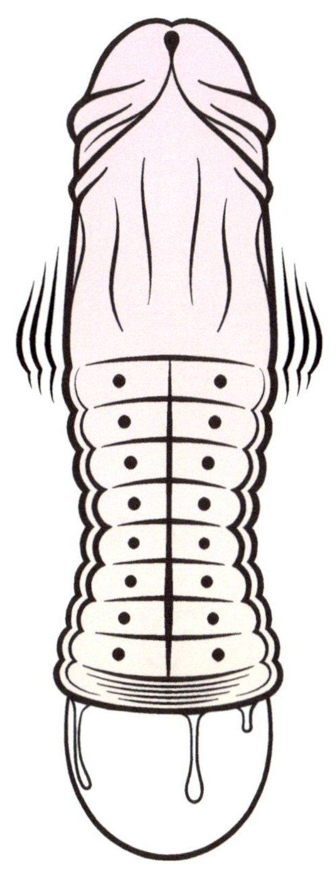

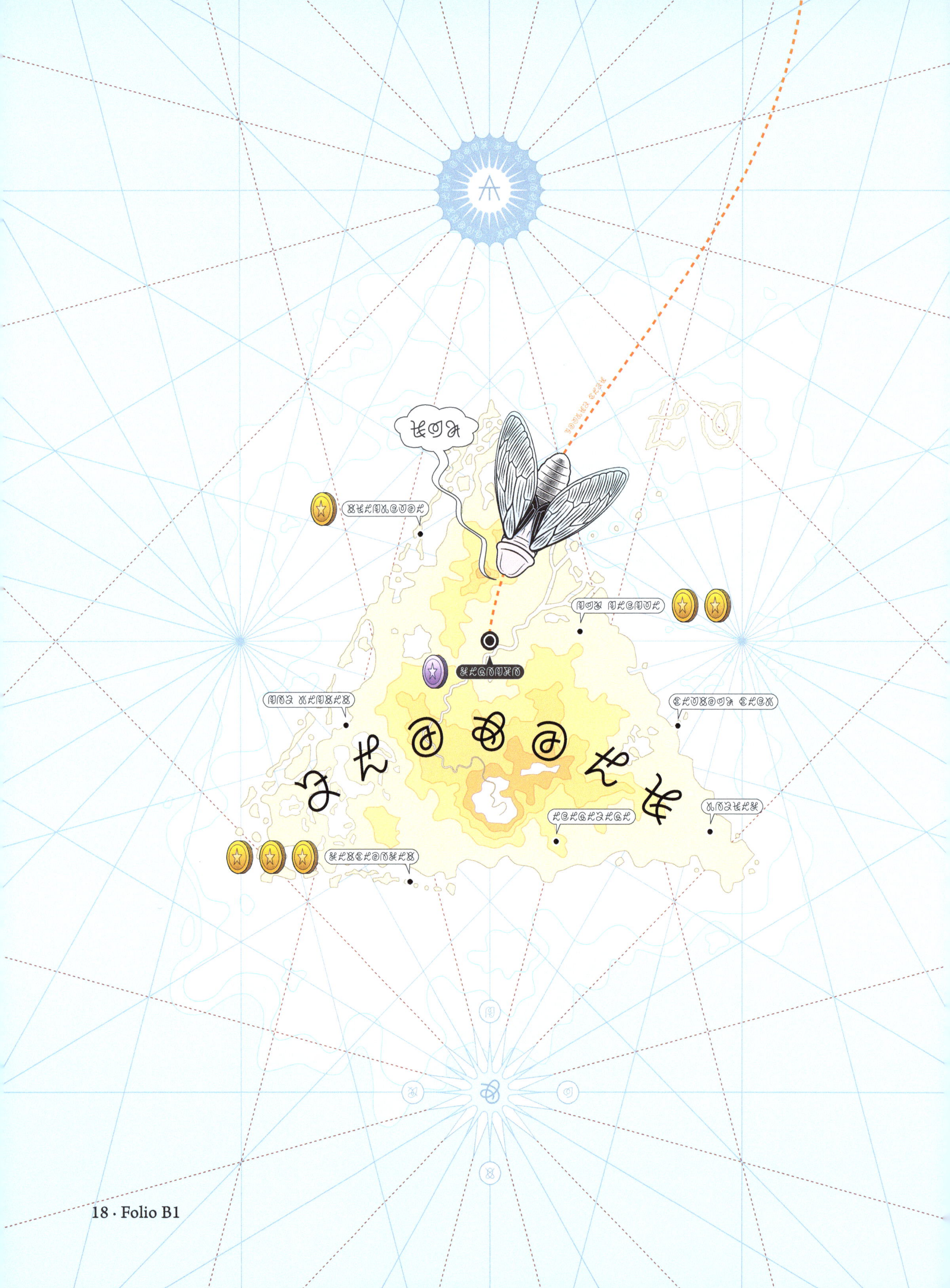

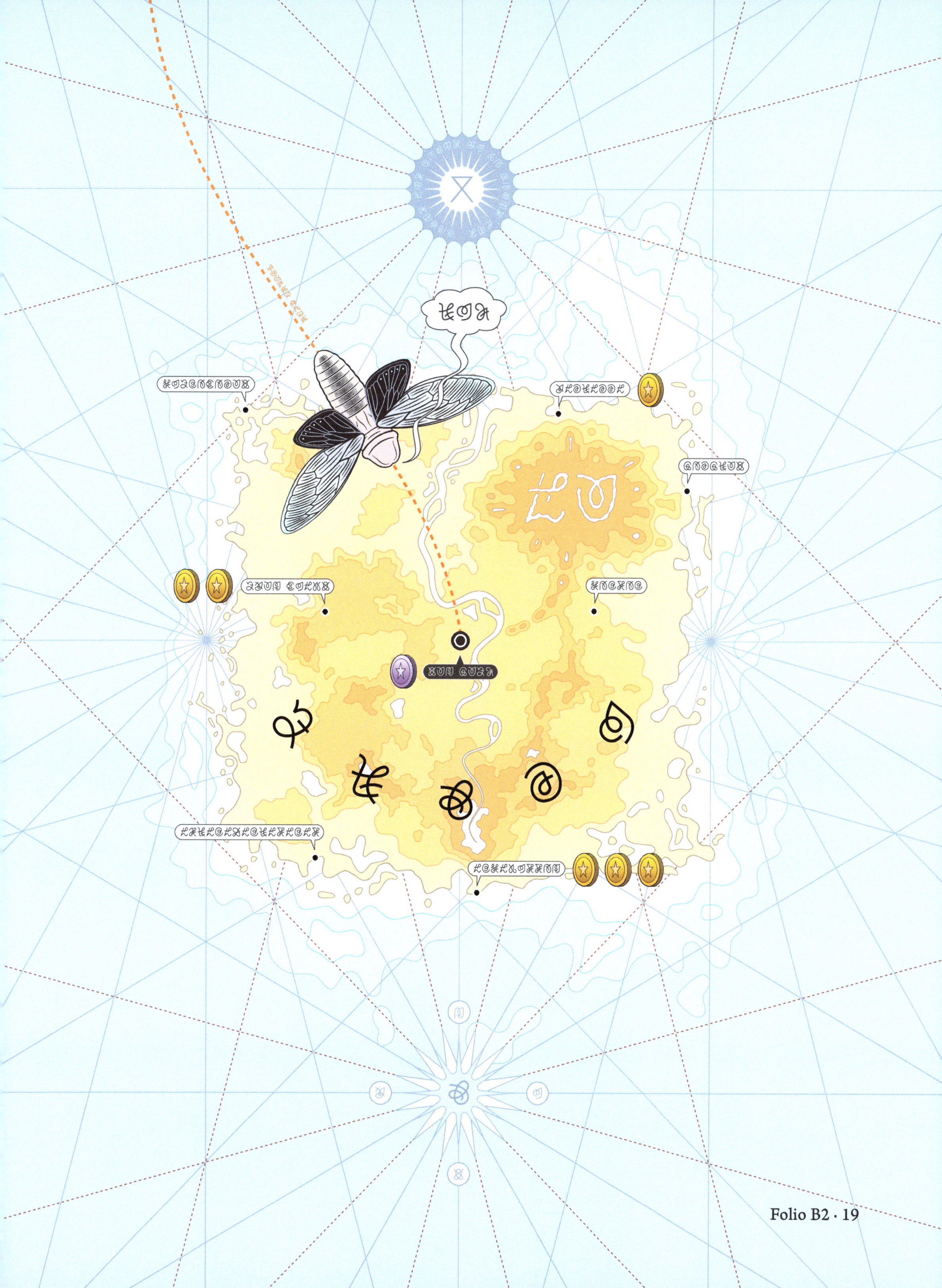

Folio B2 · 19

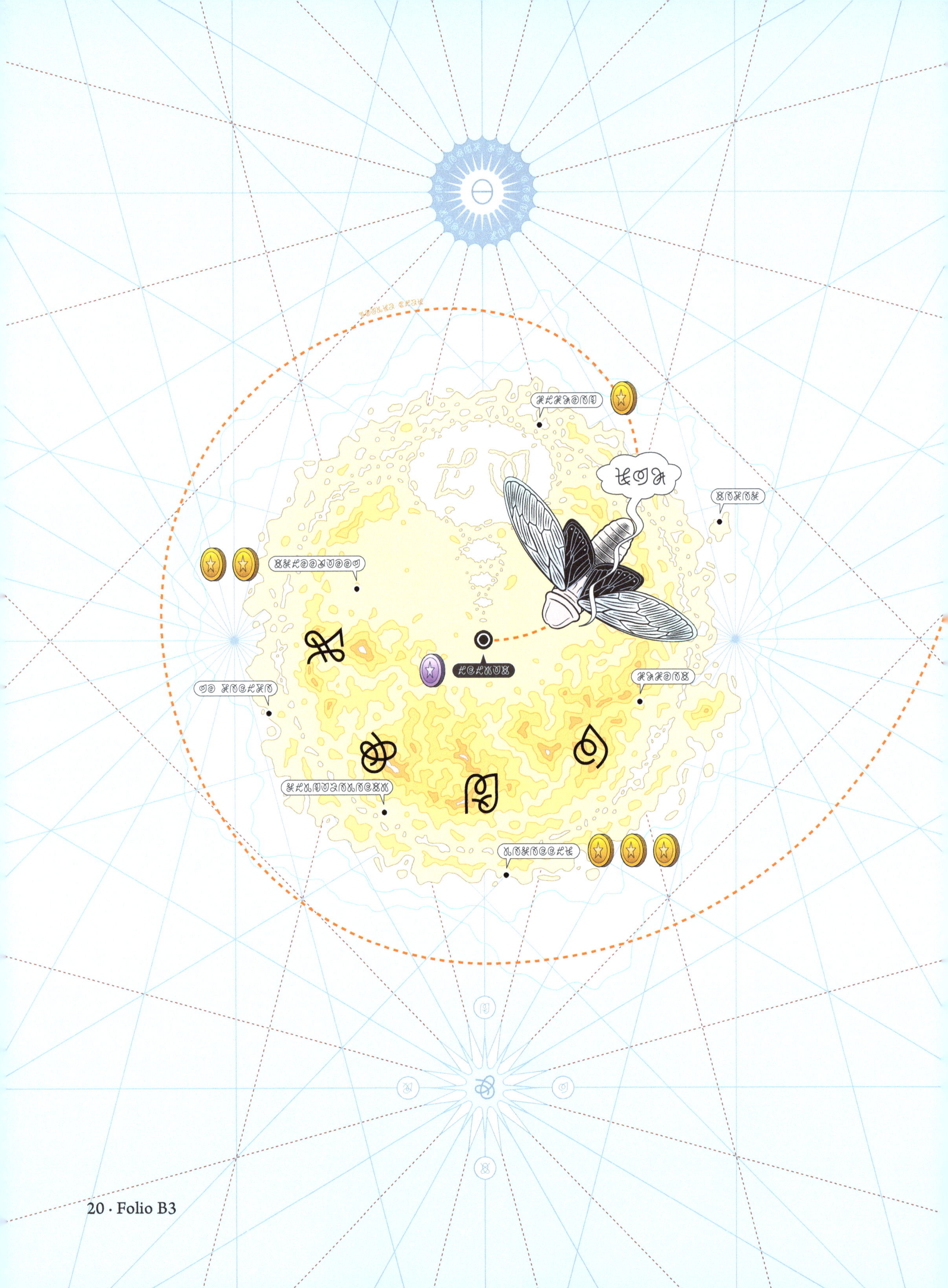

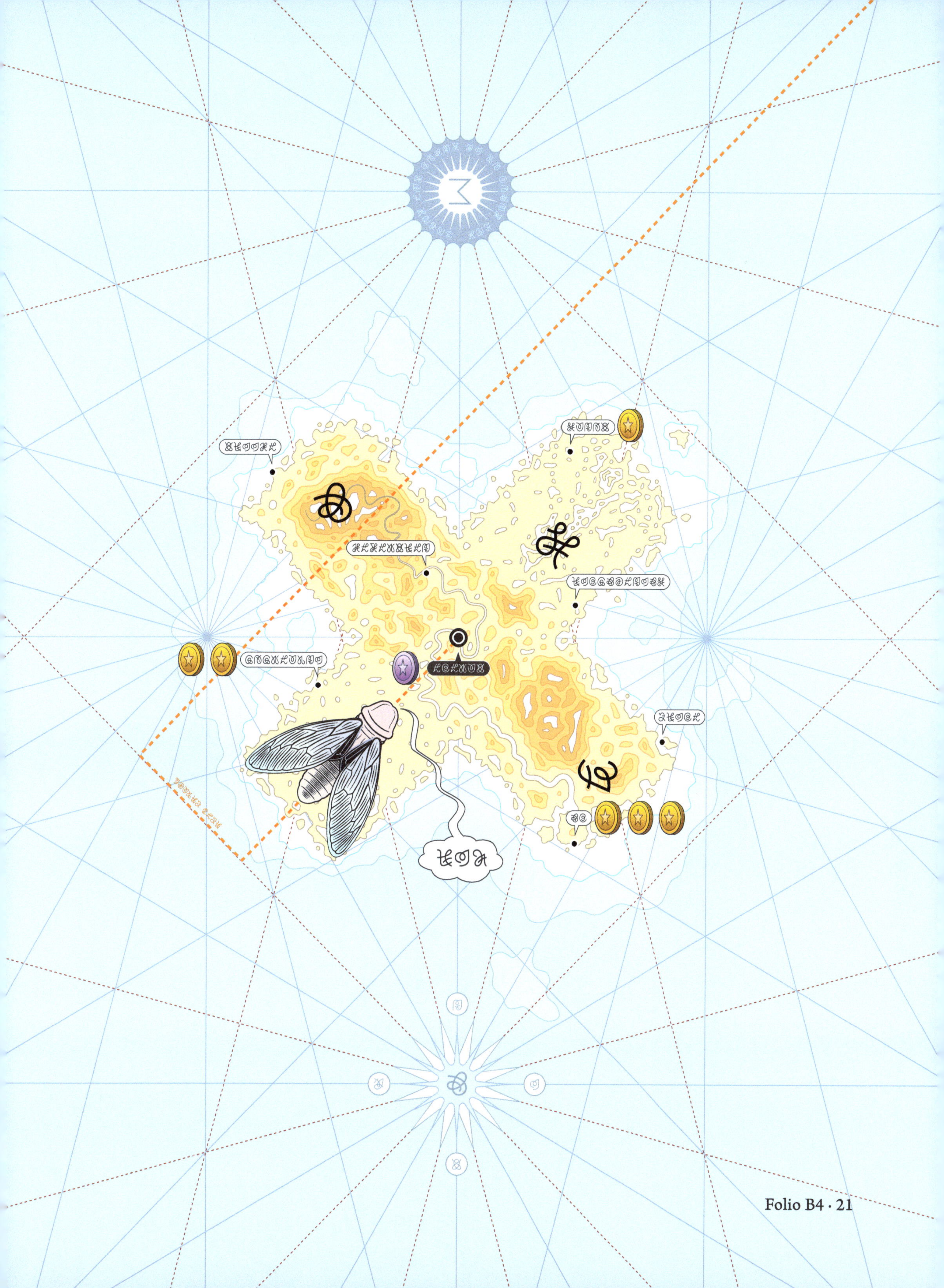

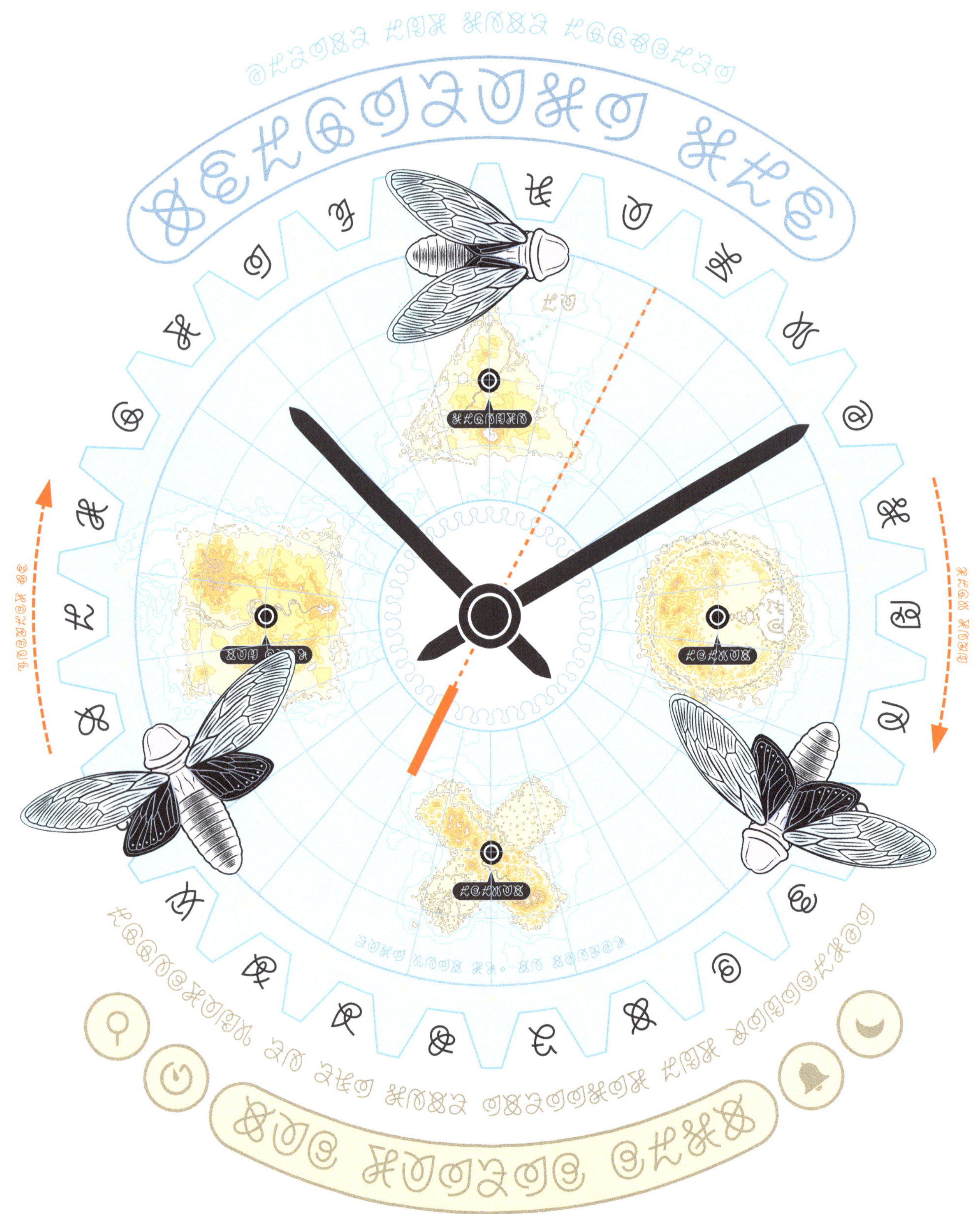

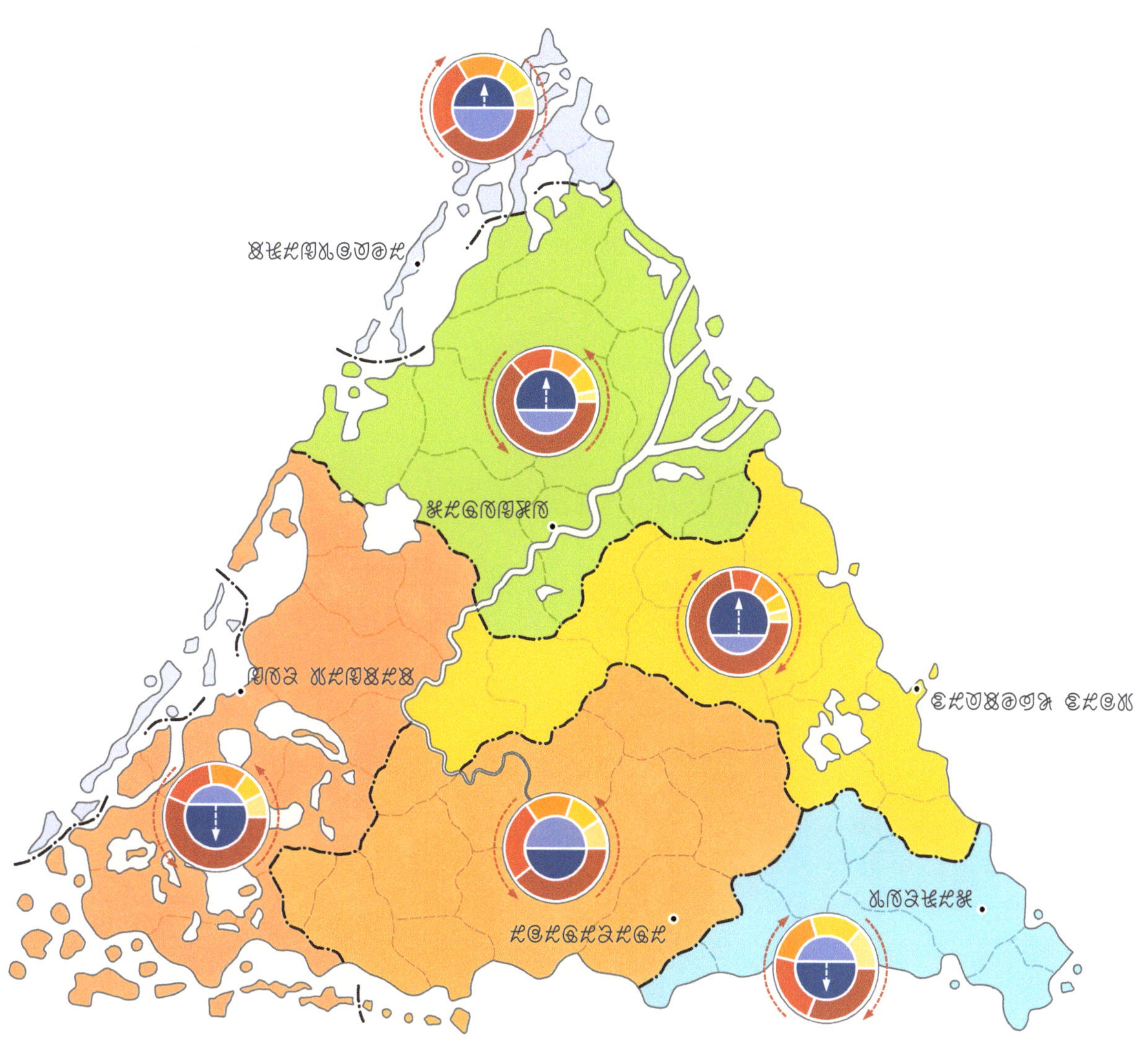

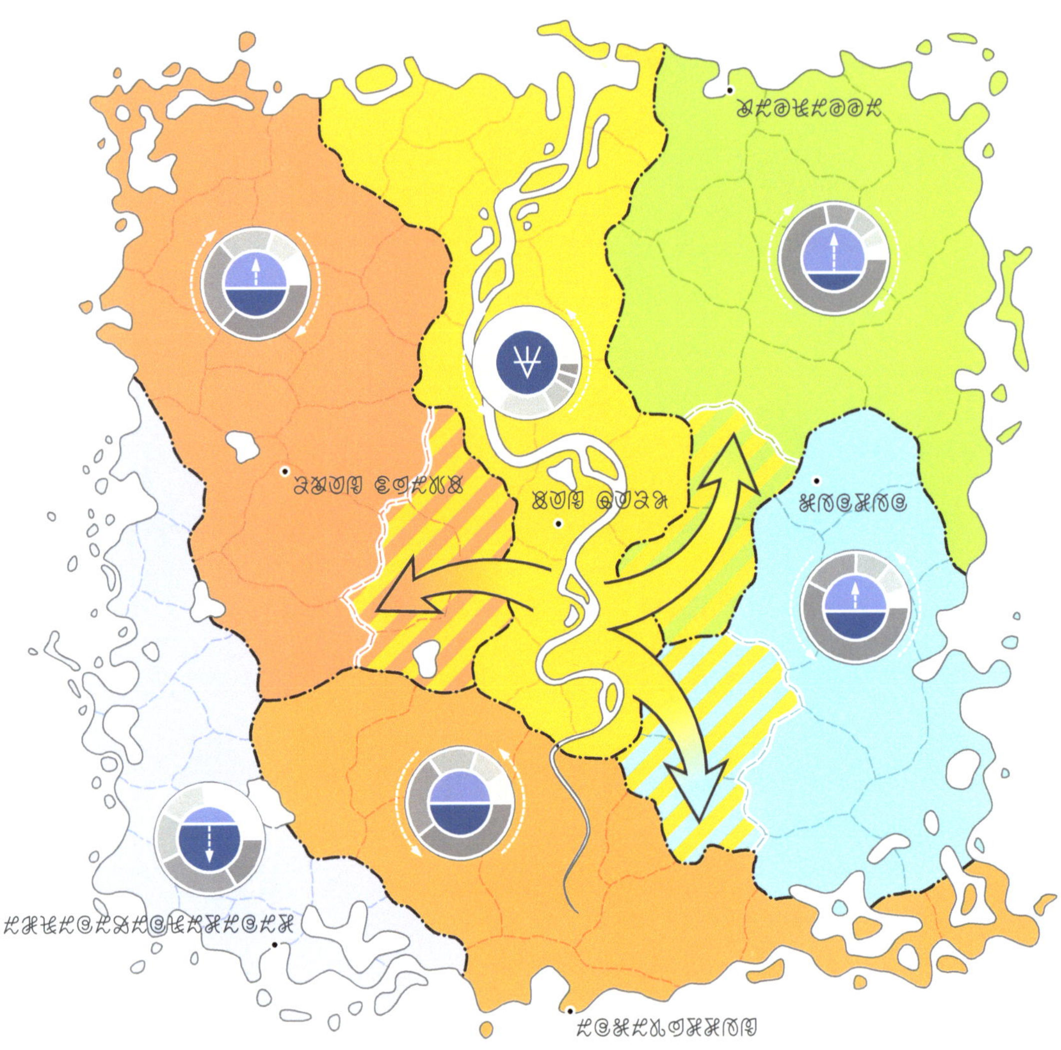

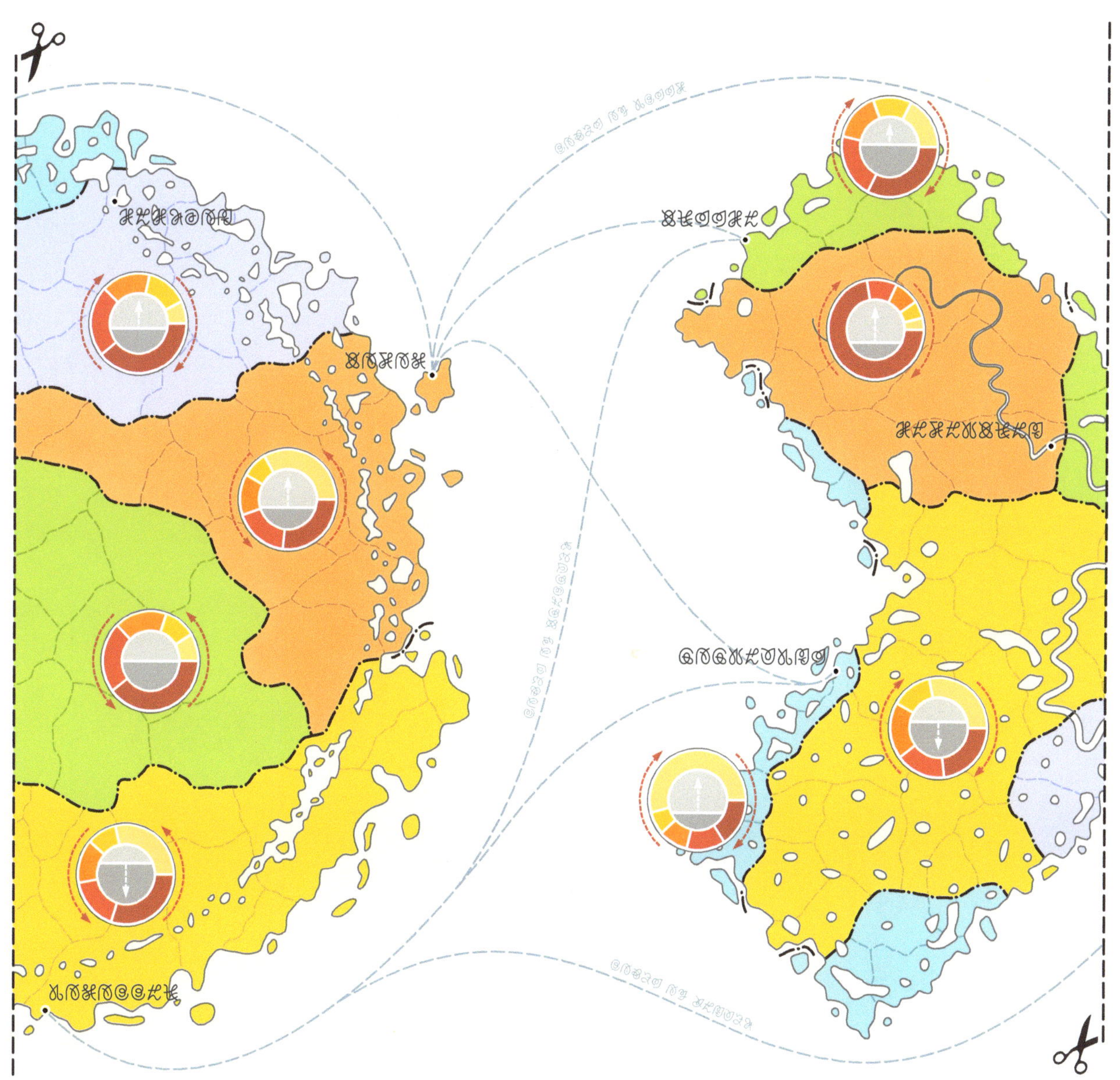

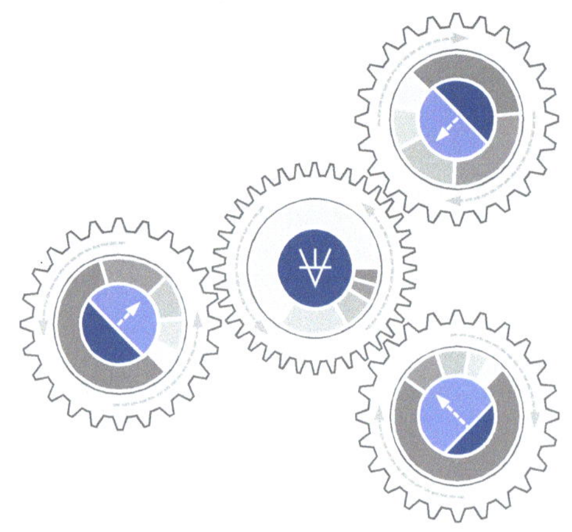

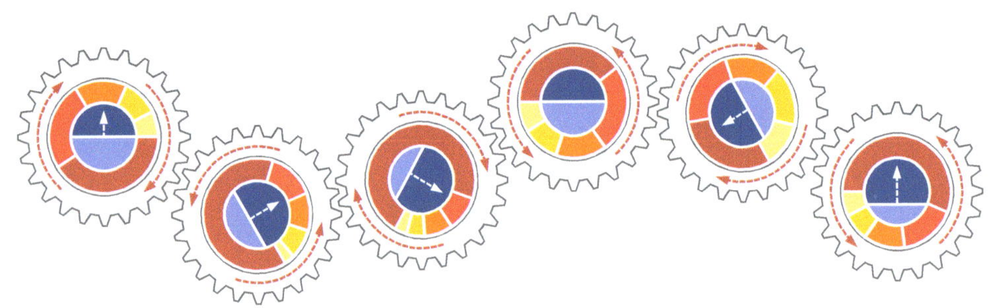

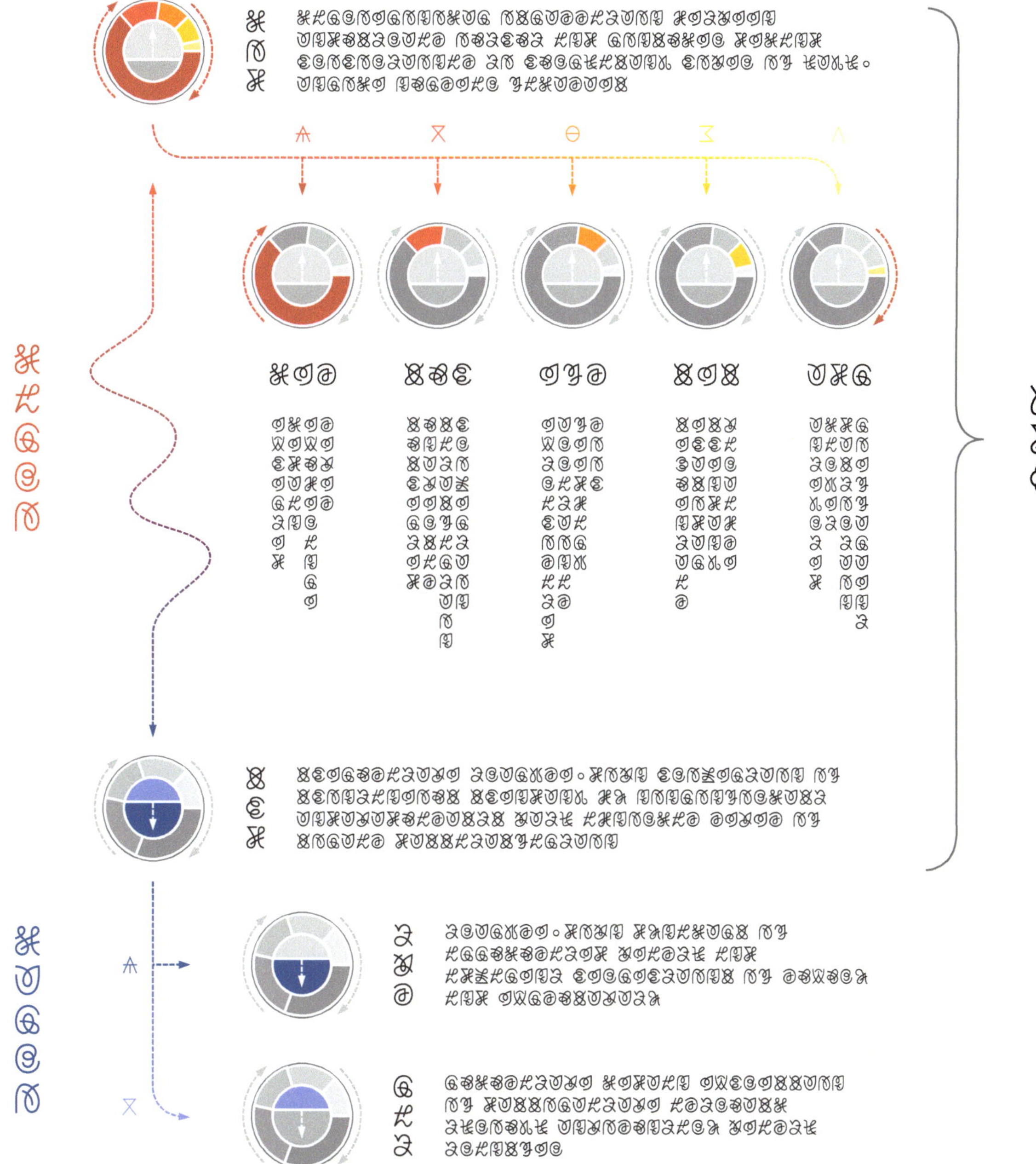

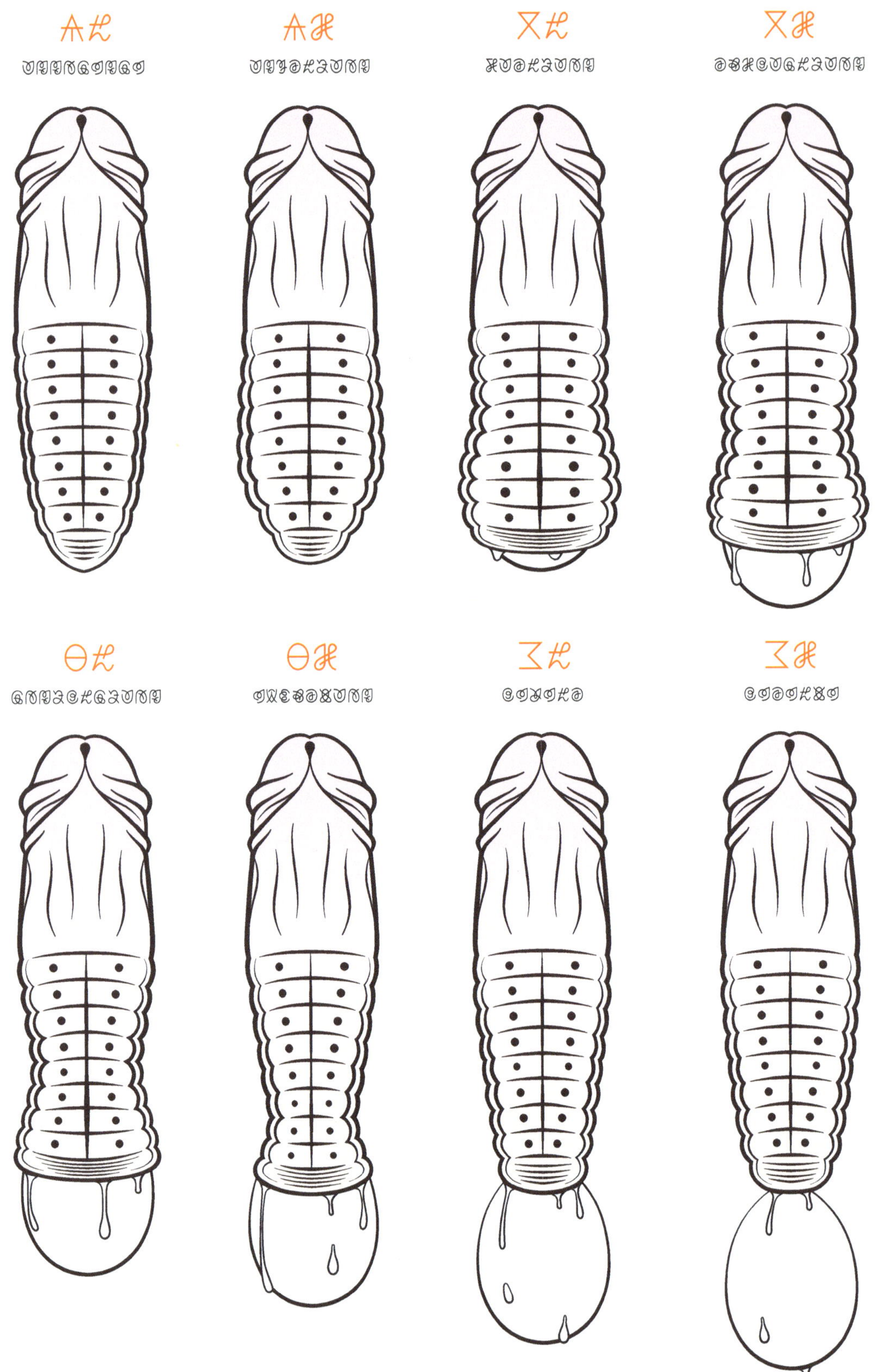

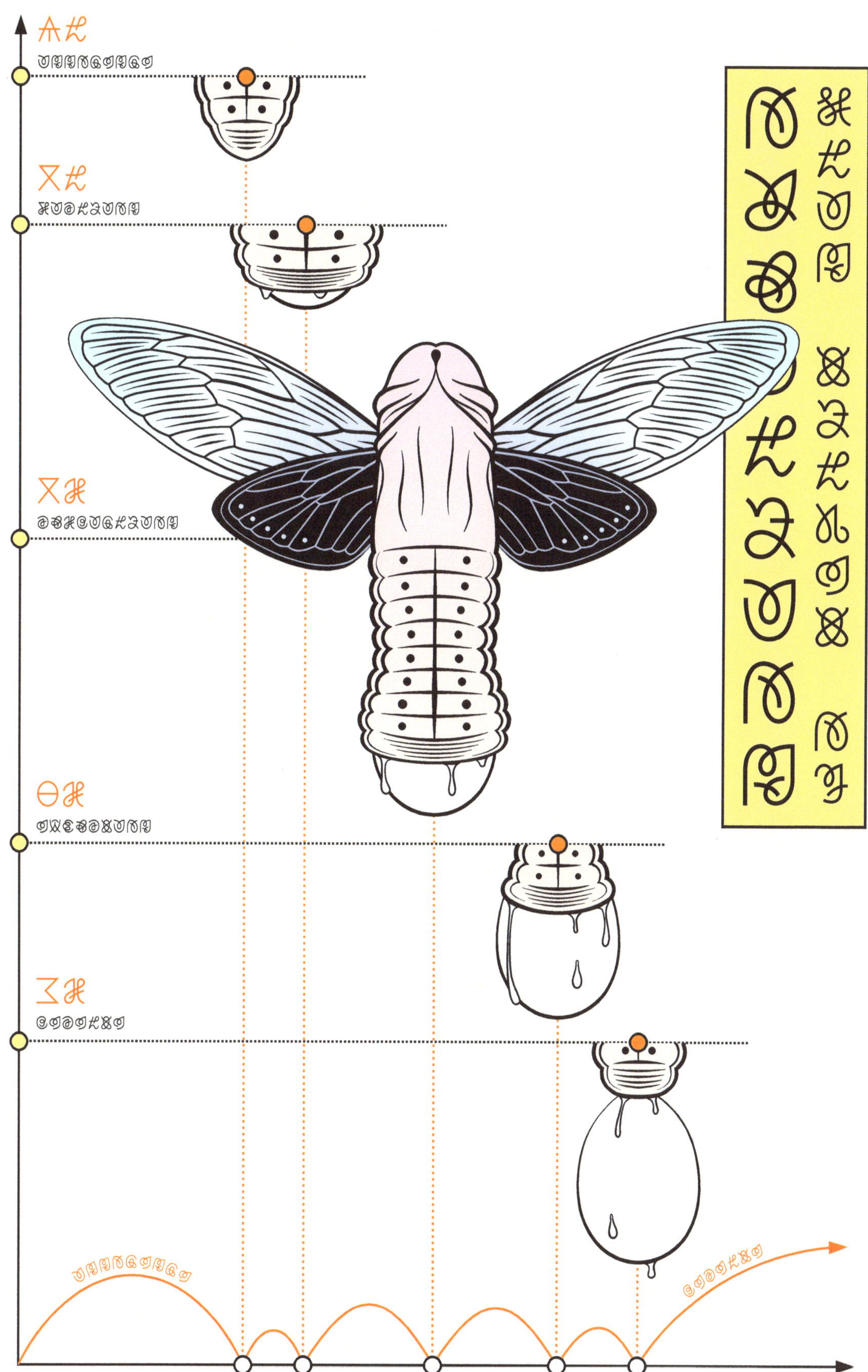

Part Three: Divulgence

Far from content with the hysterical fusion between biology and macroeconomics in his pursuit to explain the origins of the egg, the author now turns for inspiration to architecture and physics in order to depict its internal structure.

This is a genuine surprise. There's hardly a human, regardless of origin, who is not intimately familiar with the content of the egg—one of the most important and accessible food sources all over the world. Alas, the author of *The Schmetterschwanz Manuscript* seems to have misgivings about it and has obviously chosen not to trust his eyes.

The result is a vertigo-inducing amalgam of visuals that borrow symbols from architectural drawings, electromagnetic field schematics, and meteorological maps. They appear layered on top of each other, alluding to a sequential development, while the third and fourth folios suggest the entropy of the egg structure is directly dependent on the presence of an observer, an allusion that foreshadows some extravagant theories like the just emerging quantum mechanics, a branch of physics that links it to the fine art of poetry.

Why the insides of an egg would be a subject of study for those sciences remains an undisclosed secret. The textual descriptions are sparse and significantly more cryptic that those found in the previous two parts. Some of the statements border on speculative religion:

A state of self-awareness preserves the integrity of the primordial egg.

Since this part employs high levels of abstraction without any attempt at practicality, we advise caution, especially with young readers, who might be easily susceptible to sensory overload.

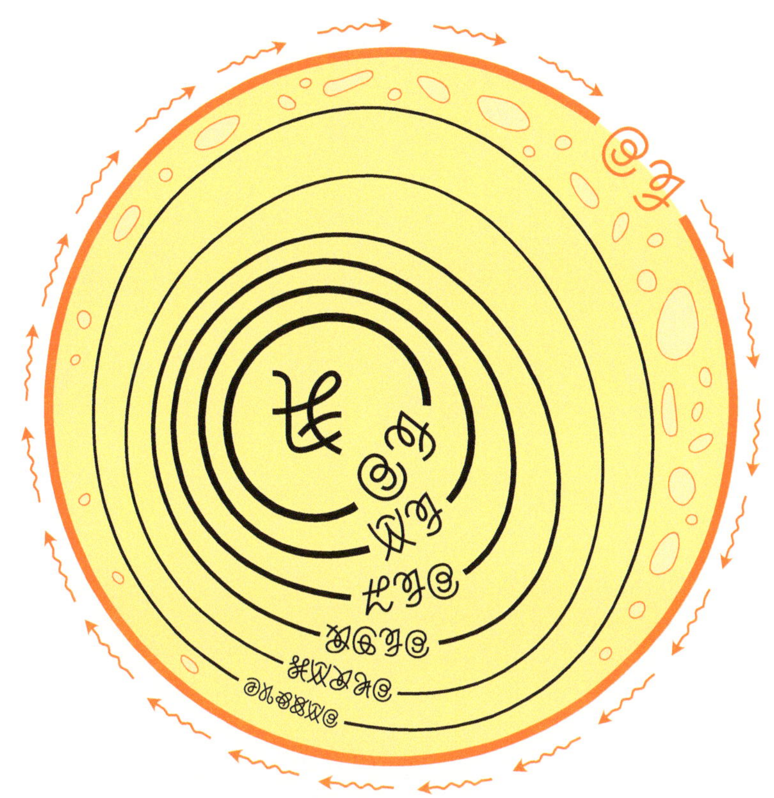

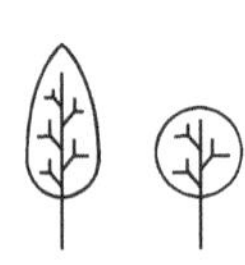

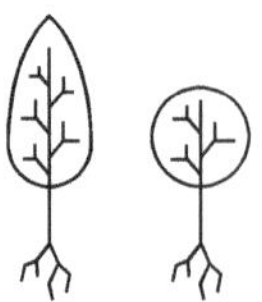

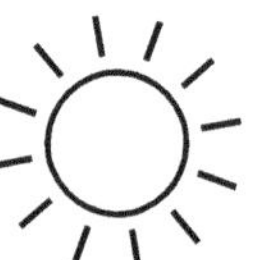

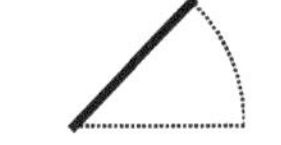

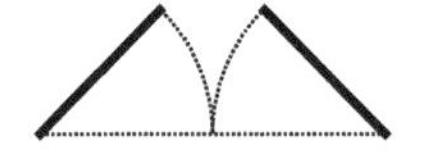

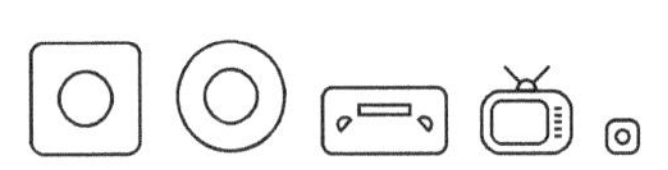

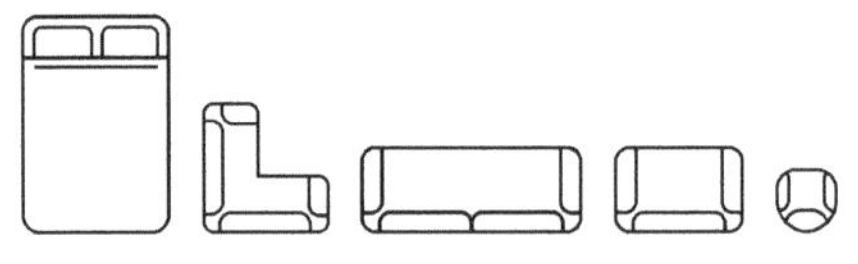

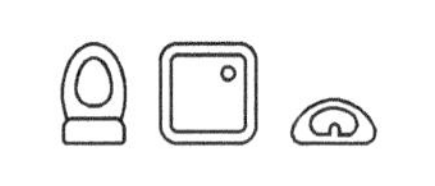

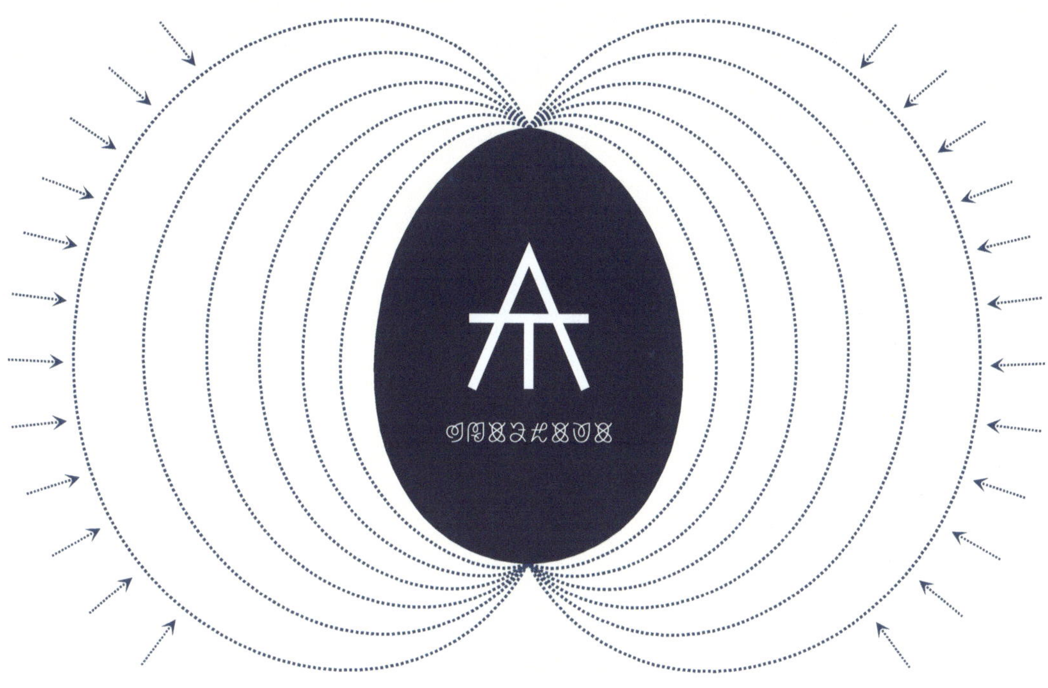

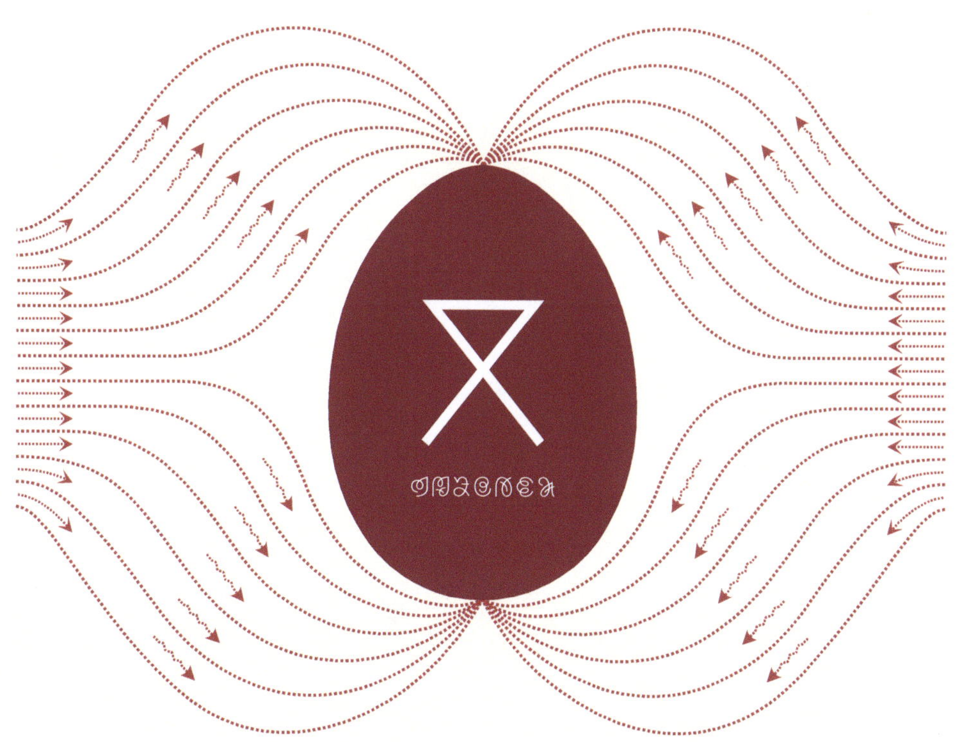

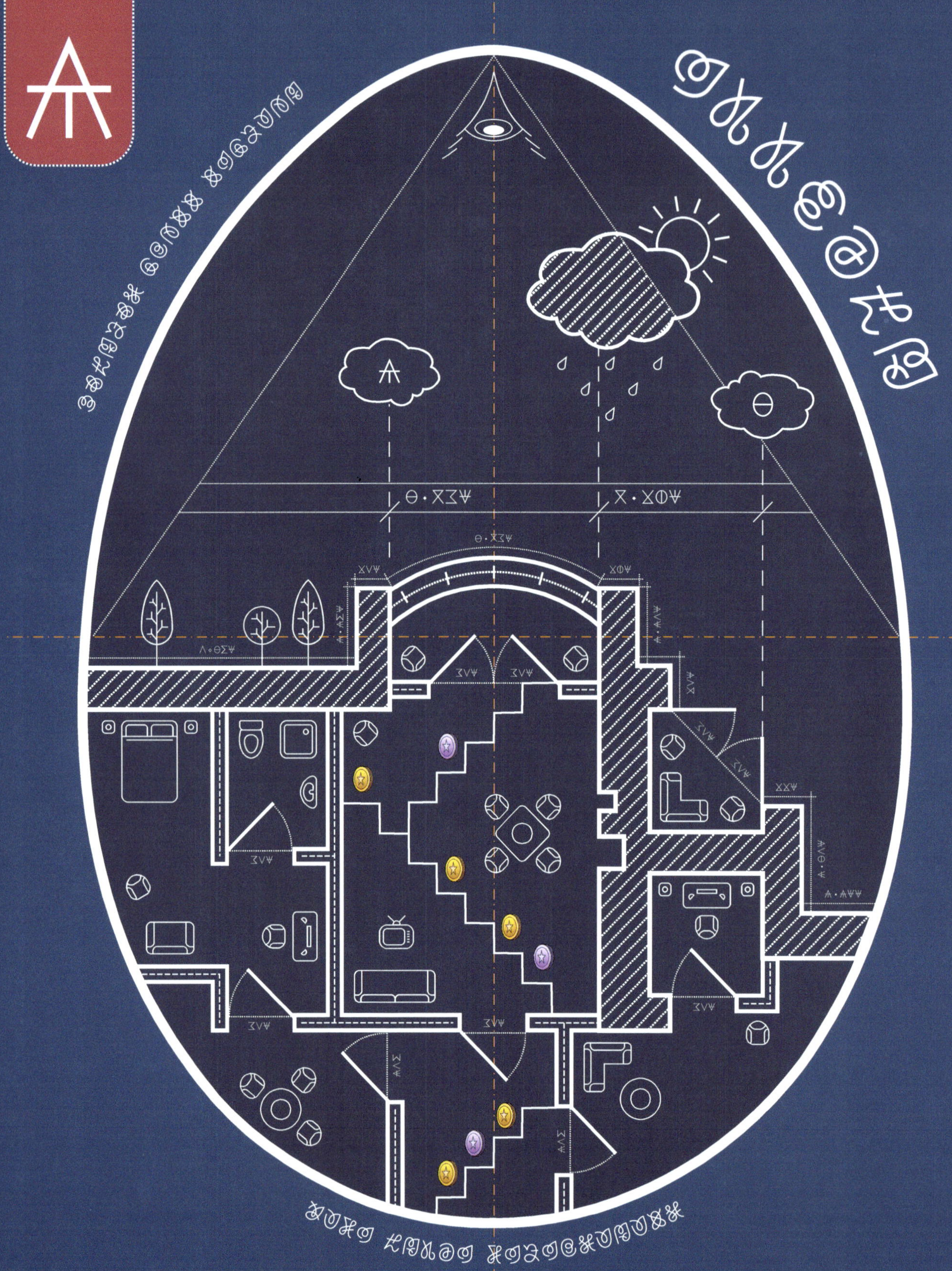

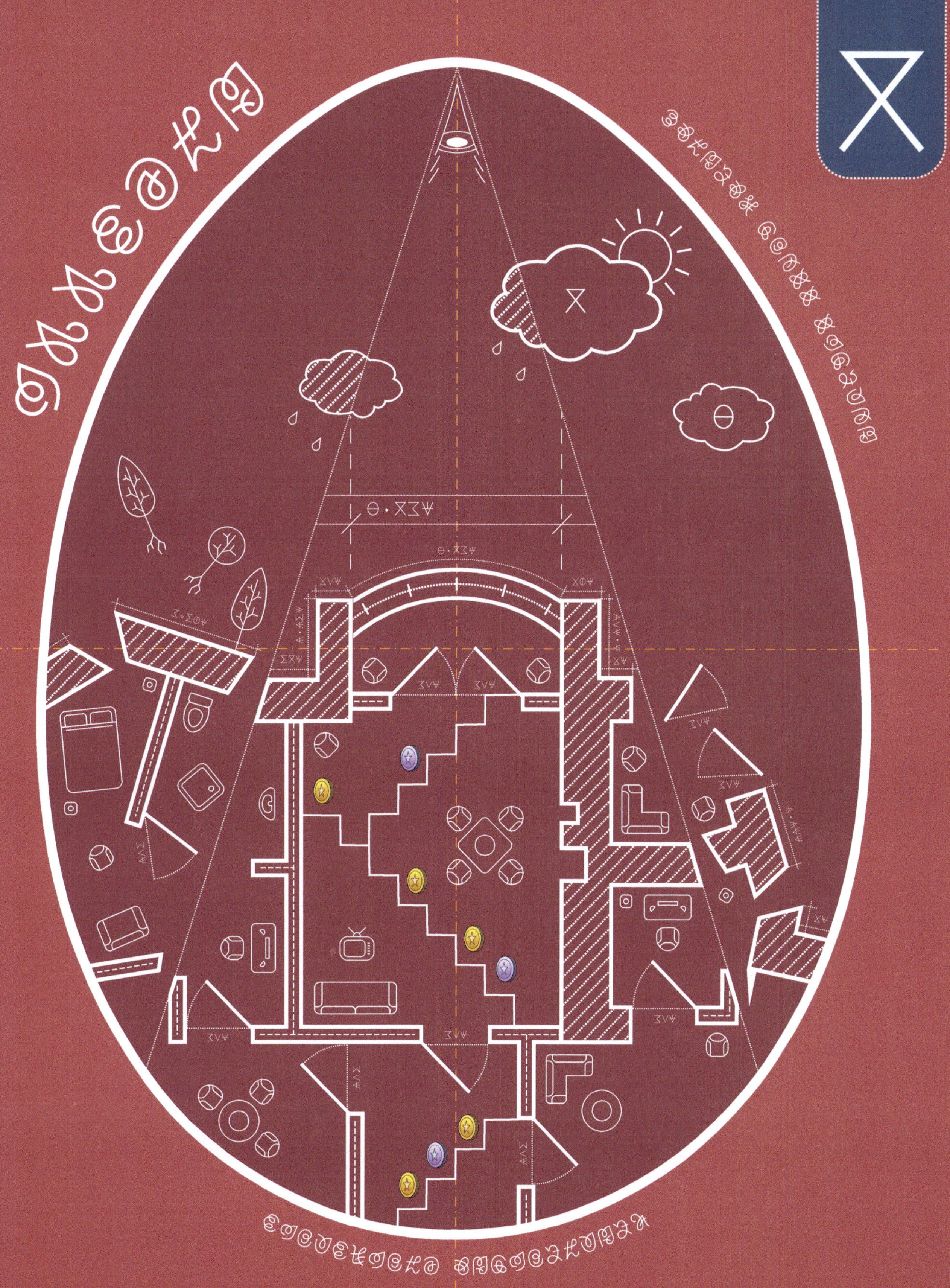

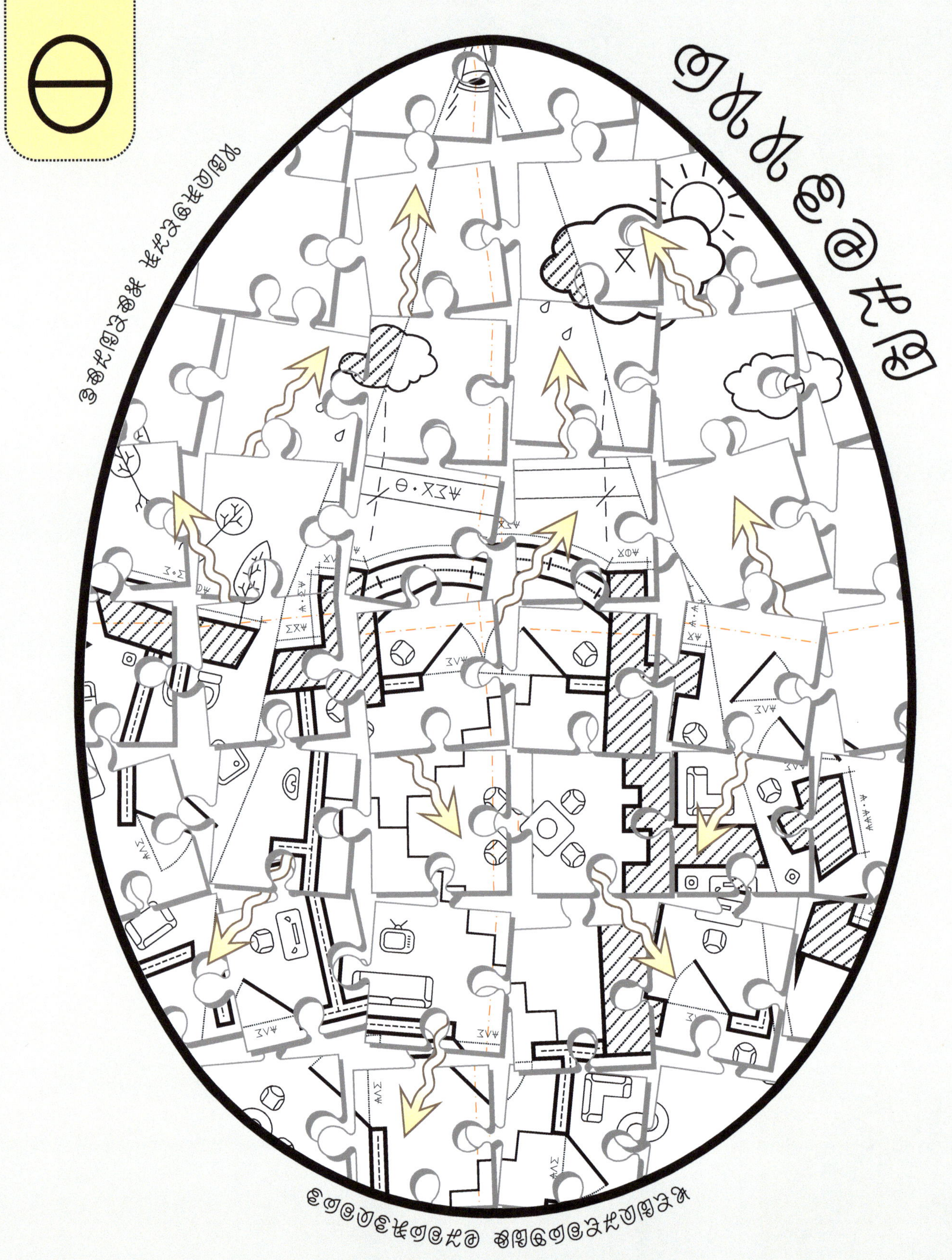

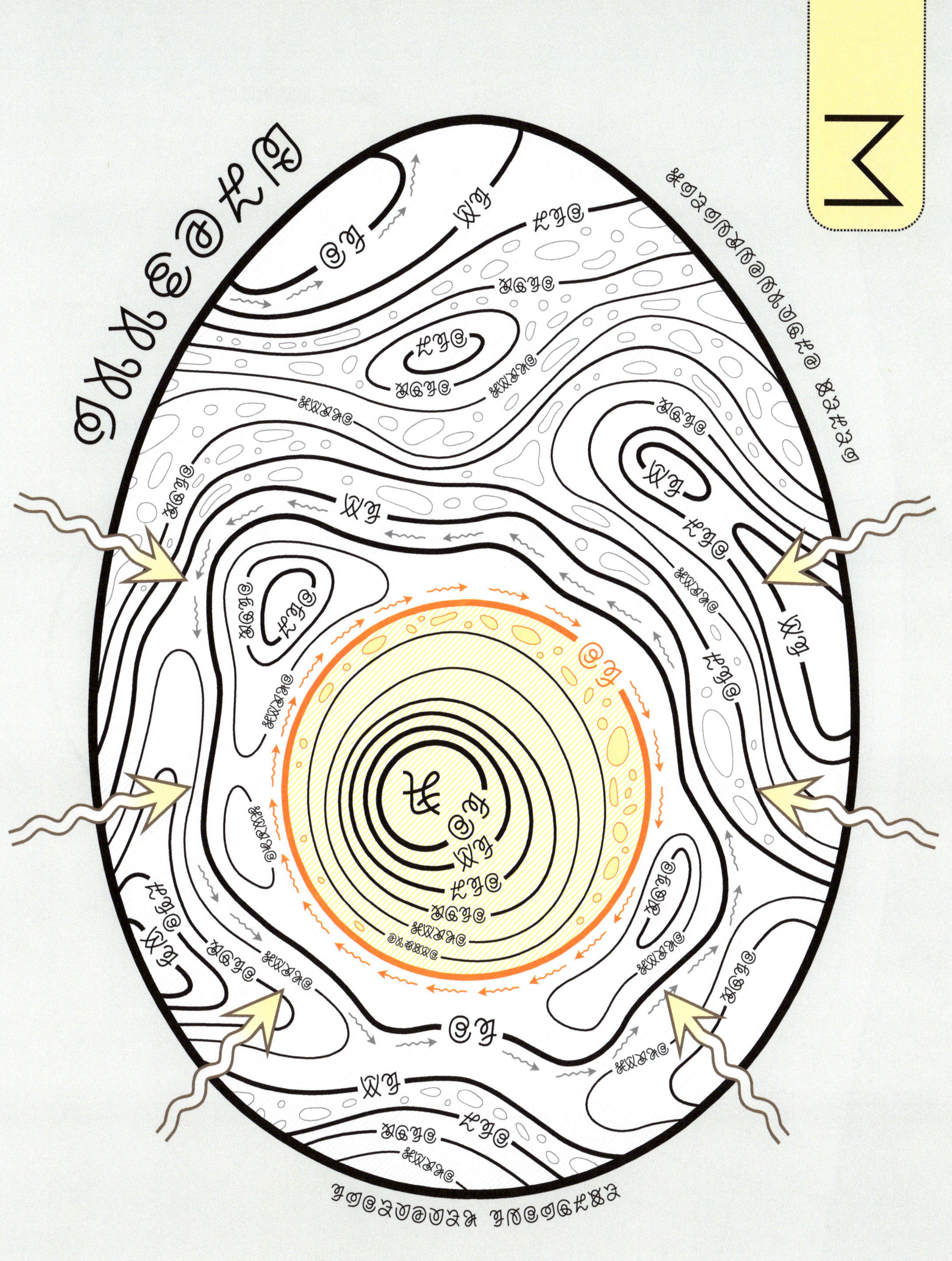

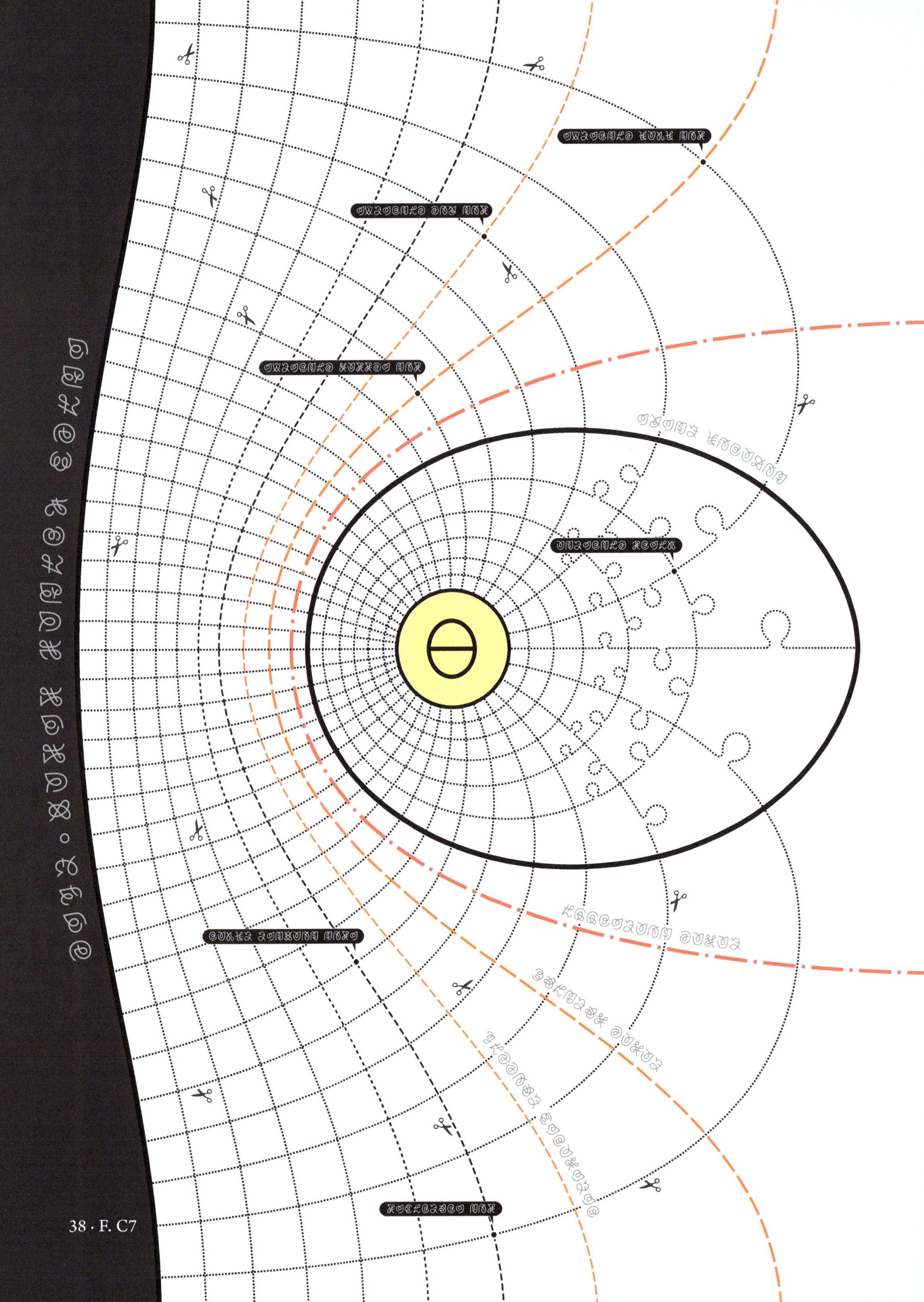

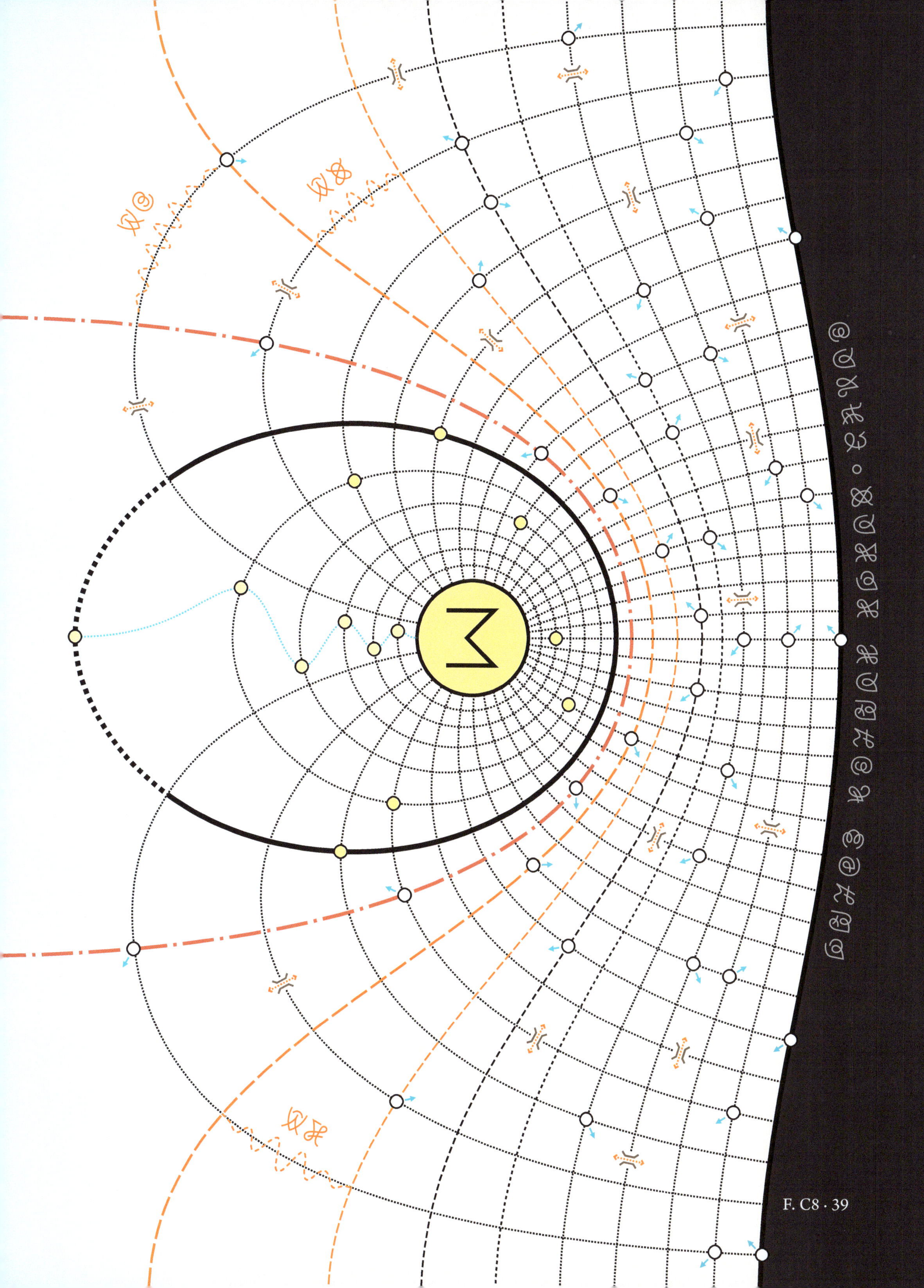

Part Four: Indulgence

The fourth folio sequence is without a doubt the most exhausting to the eyes. Our restoration team was torn between the desire to preserve the original palette and the standards of colorimetric decency. Shiny colorful stones wield enormous power over the human psyche. For reasons we struggle to explain, their price abroad often rivals that of our most precious books.

While a certain fascination with their superficial appearance is to be expected, the author doesn't stop there. The stones are reinterpreted as culinary objects, intentionally stylized to appeal to the most gluttonous instincts of the human body. The seductive provocation reaches crescendo in the packaging. The illustration on the top of the metal container depicts the already familiar airborne migratory larva laying an egg, while the label on top reads *Ave Maria*, which is without a doubt its actual name (from *ave*, being the ancient word for bird, and *maria*, derived from the ancient word for sea, *mare*).

The rim of the label is framed with nutritional information and a list of ingredients: wheat flour, butter, milk, sugar, eggs, salt, ammonium bicarbonate, sodium bicarbonate, vanilla (the last being an unknown, probably psychotropic substance). It's not immediately apparent what is the function of such a list when the actual method of preparation is completely missing. We can only assume that in primitive societies this extra information was usually transmitted orally or even worse—its dissemination might have been a taboo, as is observed among some peasants in the North, who are so sentimentally attached to their own recipes that they consider them parts of their human identity.

The box includes a kit of specialized utensils whose function can't be deciphered. There is no information on how they are supposed to be handled and even if there were, any attempt to use them would most certainly lead to serious injury.

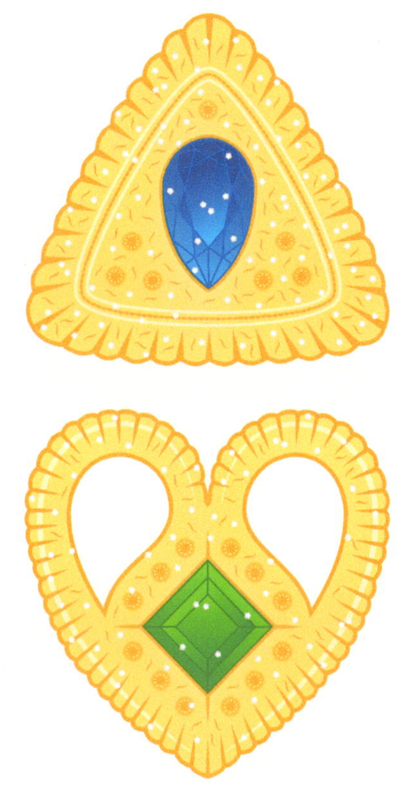

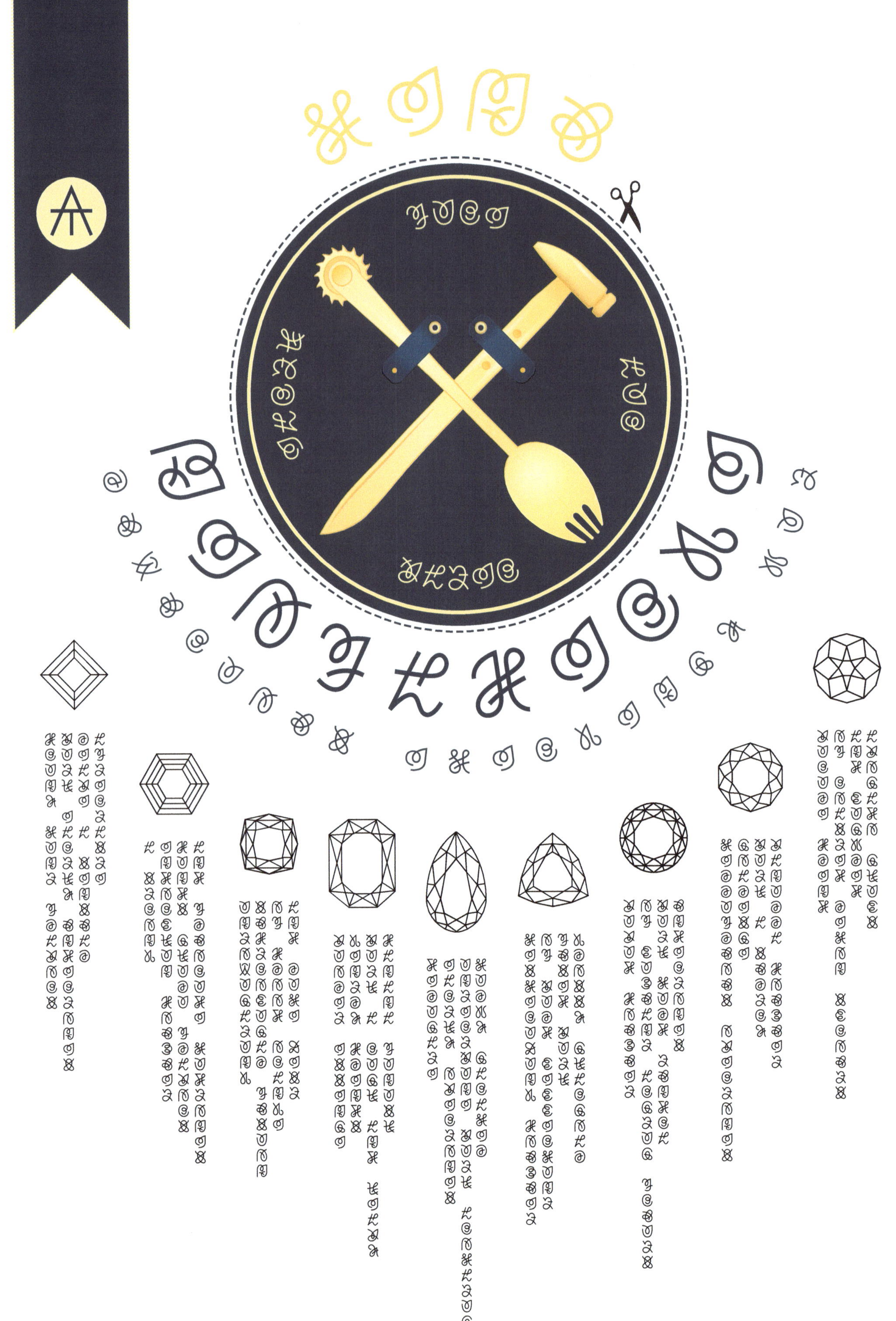

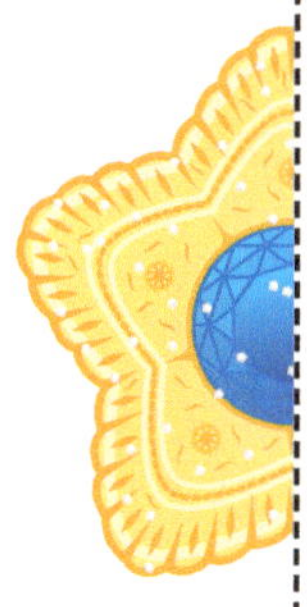

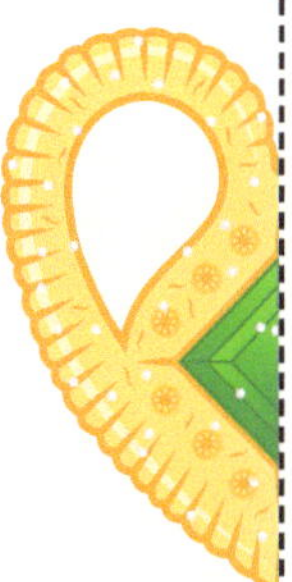

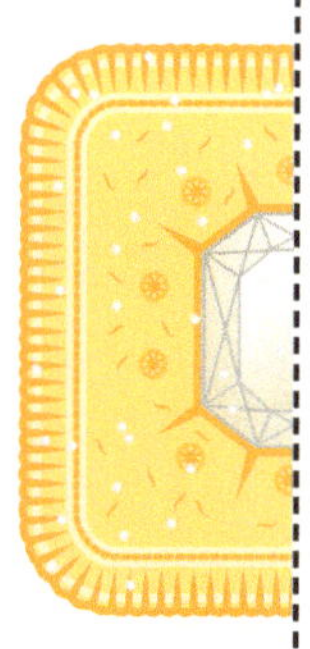

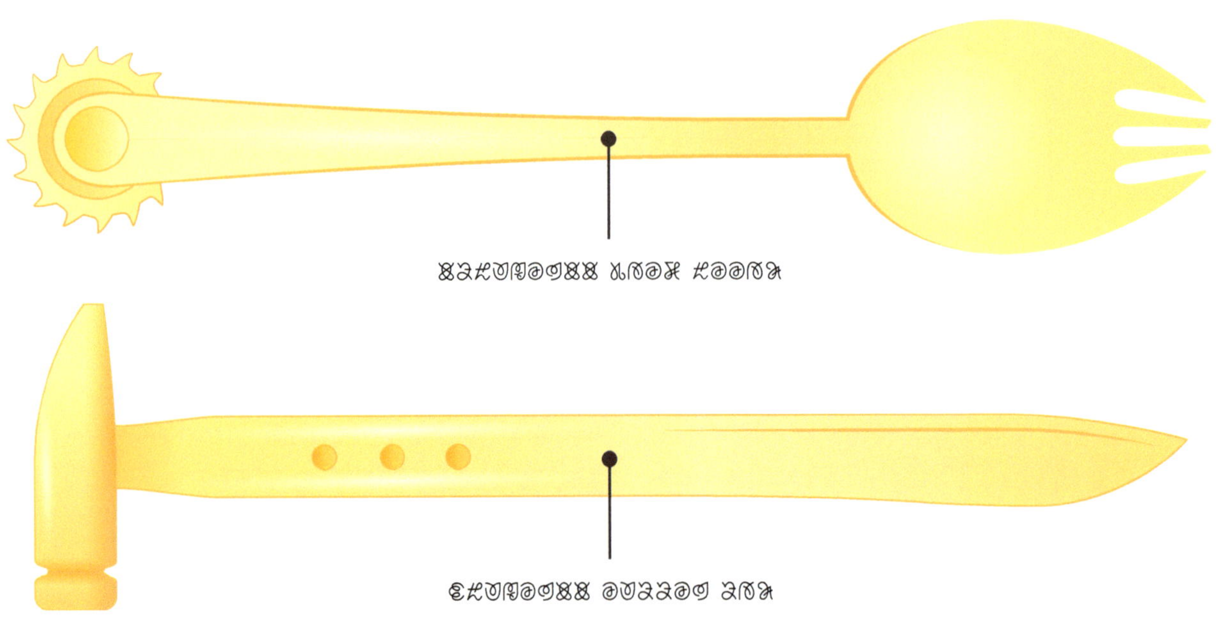

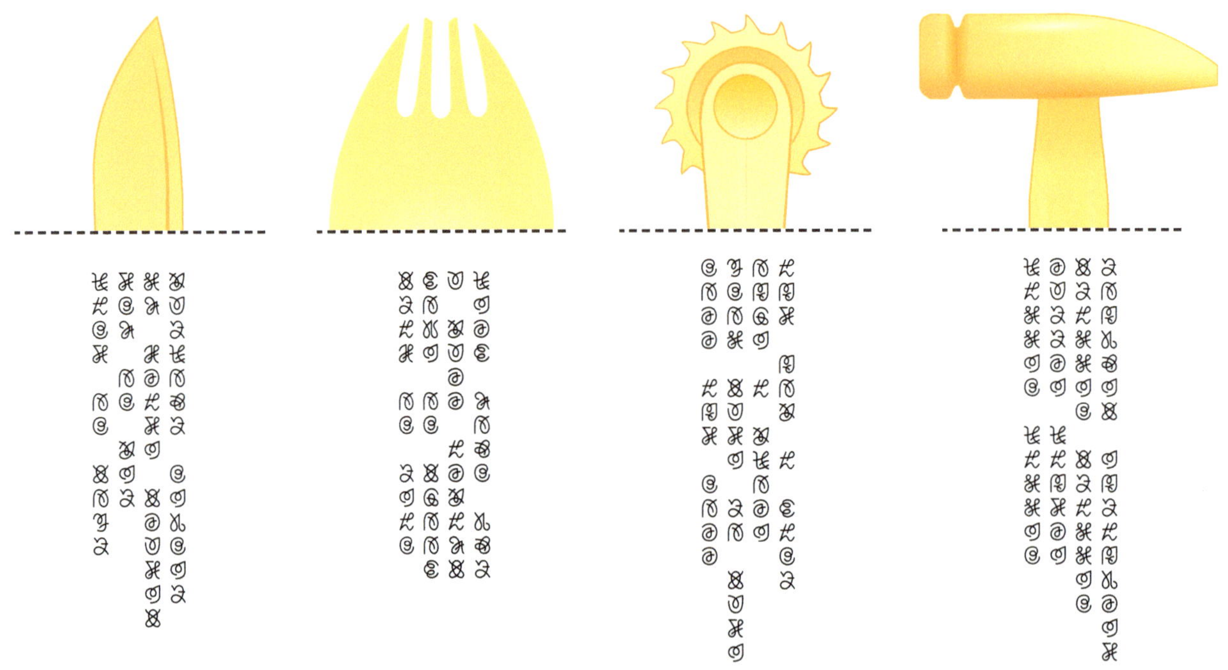

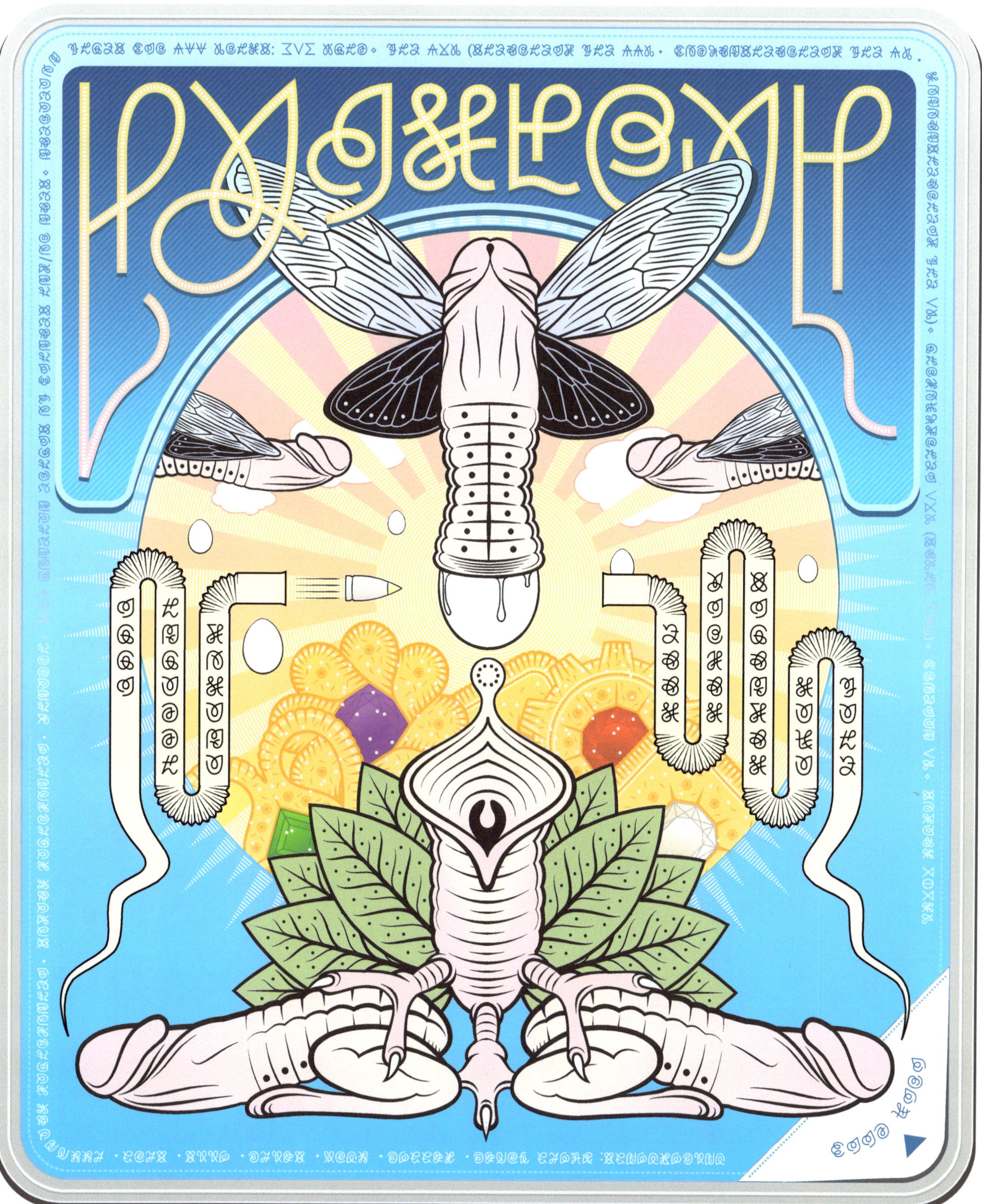

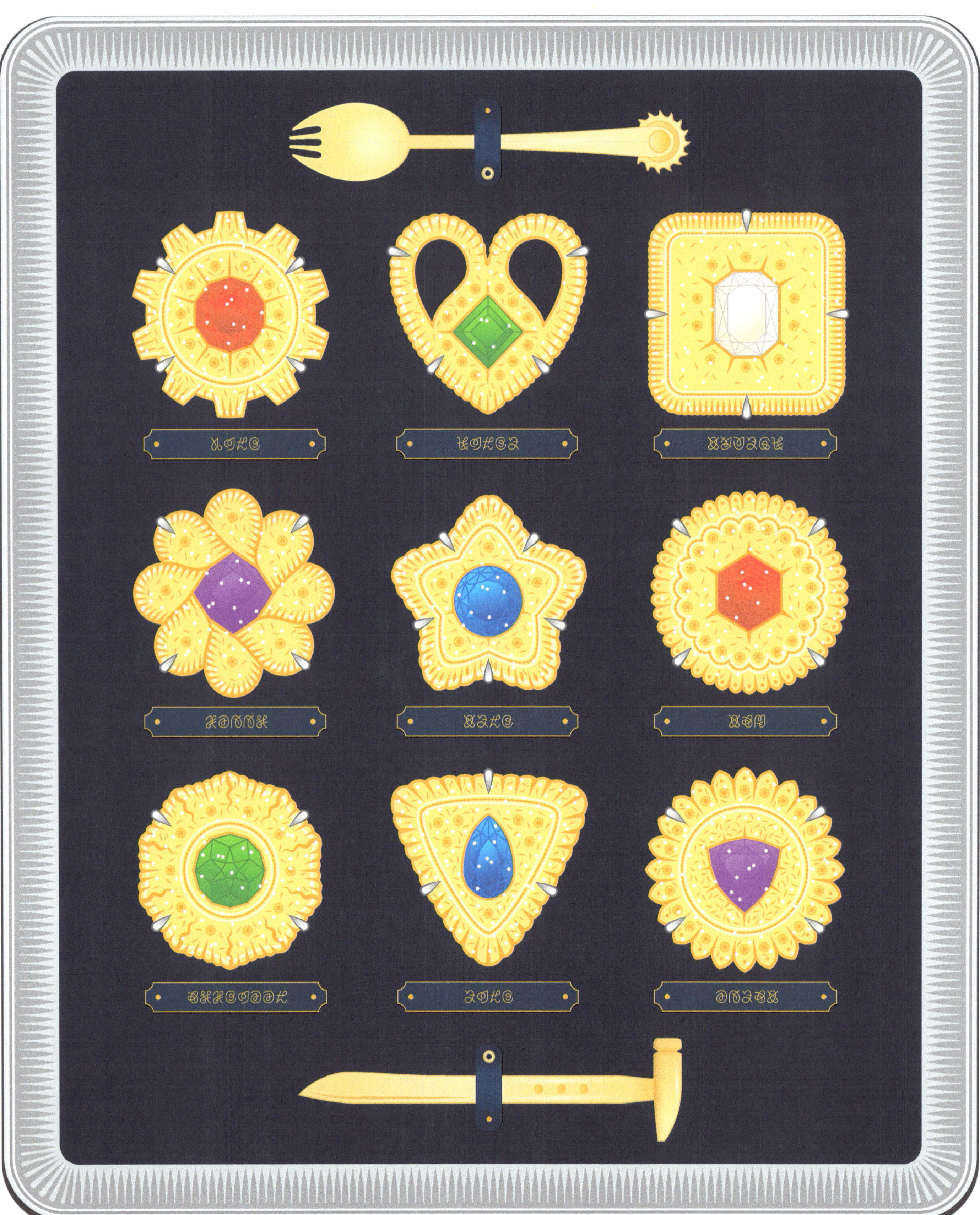

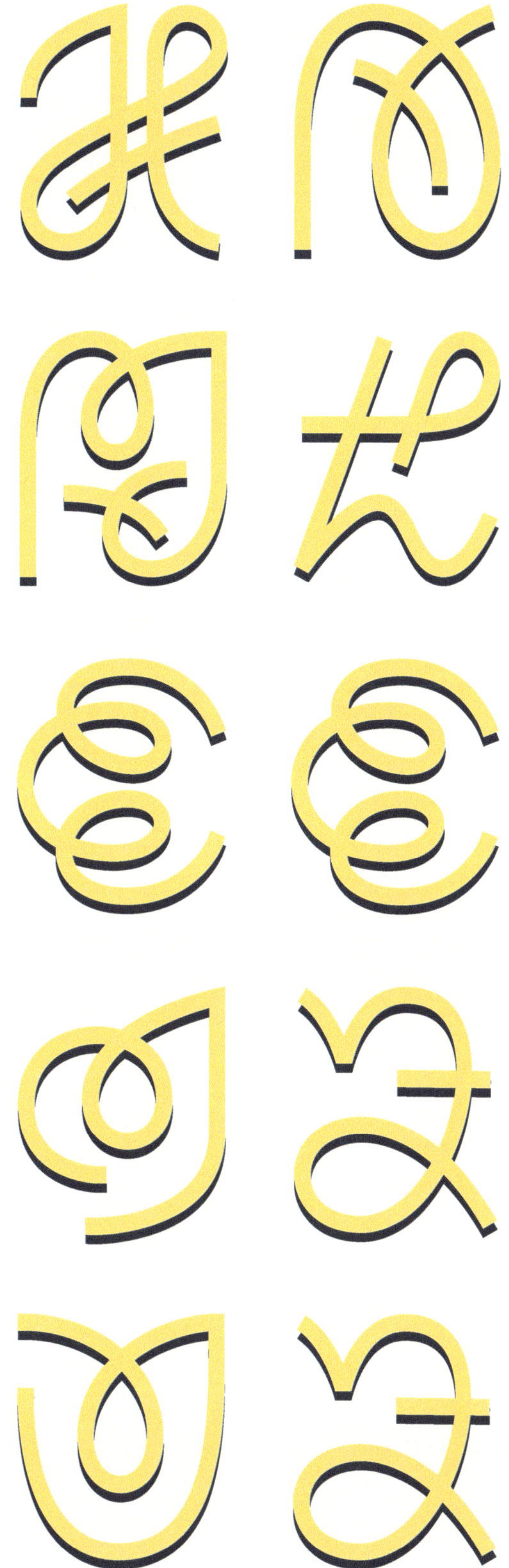

Part Five: Detergence

No dictionary in our possession has an entry for the word *detergence*. The closest match is of course *detergent*, and the similarity between the two implies a cleaning process. Depending on your point of view, it is either ironic or macabre that the leading illustration is of a bloody, foaming mouth.

How is poisoning related to cleansing remains unclear, but there are cultures whose religion is based on the belief that in their current bodies, human beings are inherently unclean, and the only path to cleanliness is through death and the consequent resurrection on a higher plane, which they call *heaven*.

In this context, the appearance of a torture device on the next few folios is not a surprise. Equipped with sharp rotating drills and a flexible handle, it certainly looks deadly and might have been employed in some form of ritualistic sacrifice.

The function of this device seems to be aided by a crystalline paste contained in a tube, although its branding *Drool'n'Glitter* seems unnecessarily acerbic.

The interpretative cryptologists who worked on the manuscript for nearly a decade all agree that the last image is connected to the artist's idea of the Afterlife. They have assured us that, although such an assumption might appear strange at first thought, the mathematical models they employed during the colorimetric and proportional analysis of the composition all suggest that the depicted device is impossible to build and cannot exist in the physical world as we know it.

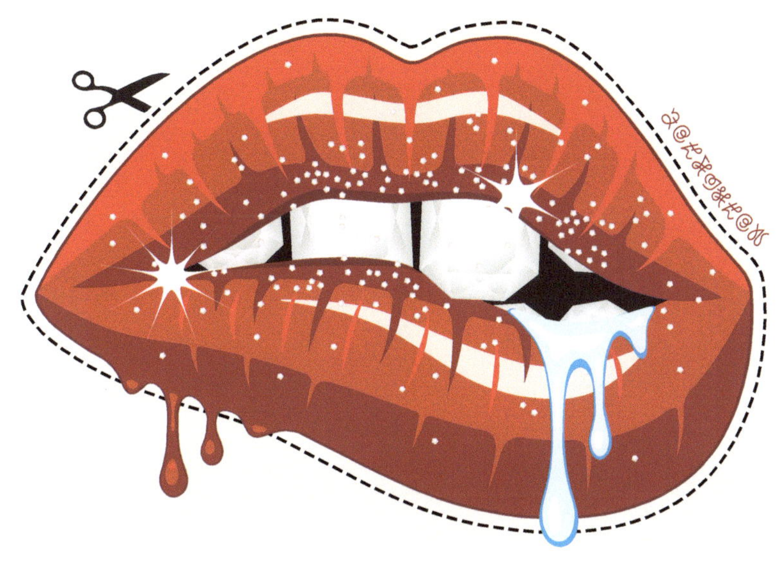

49

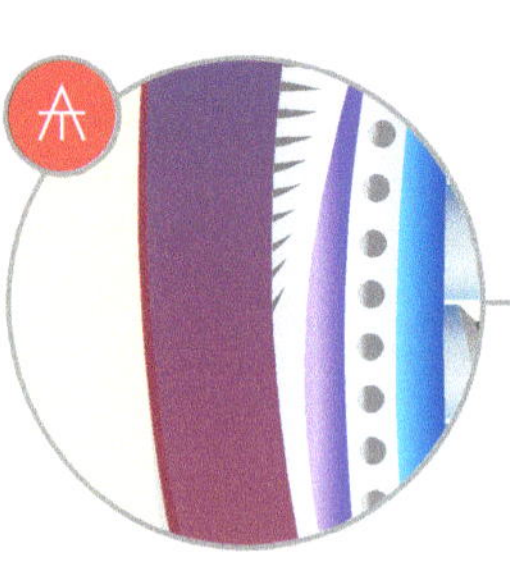
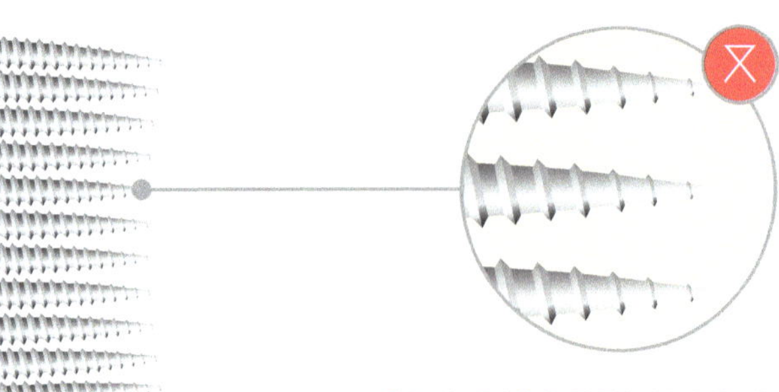
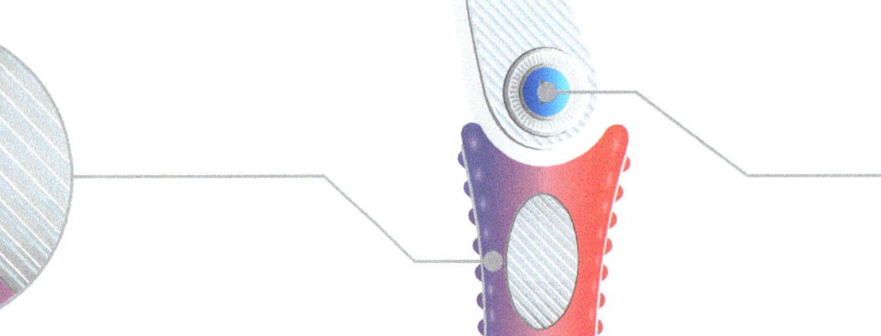
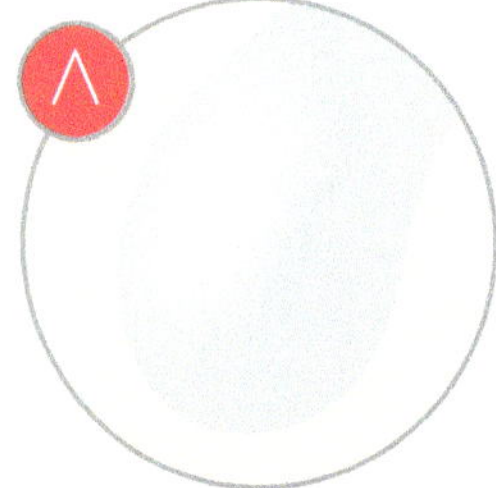
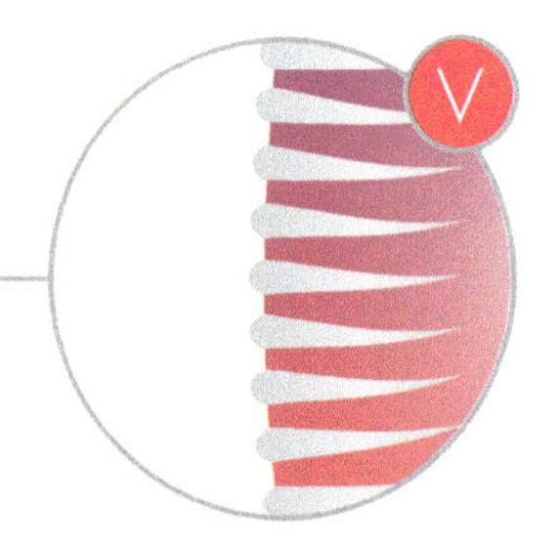

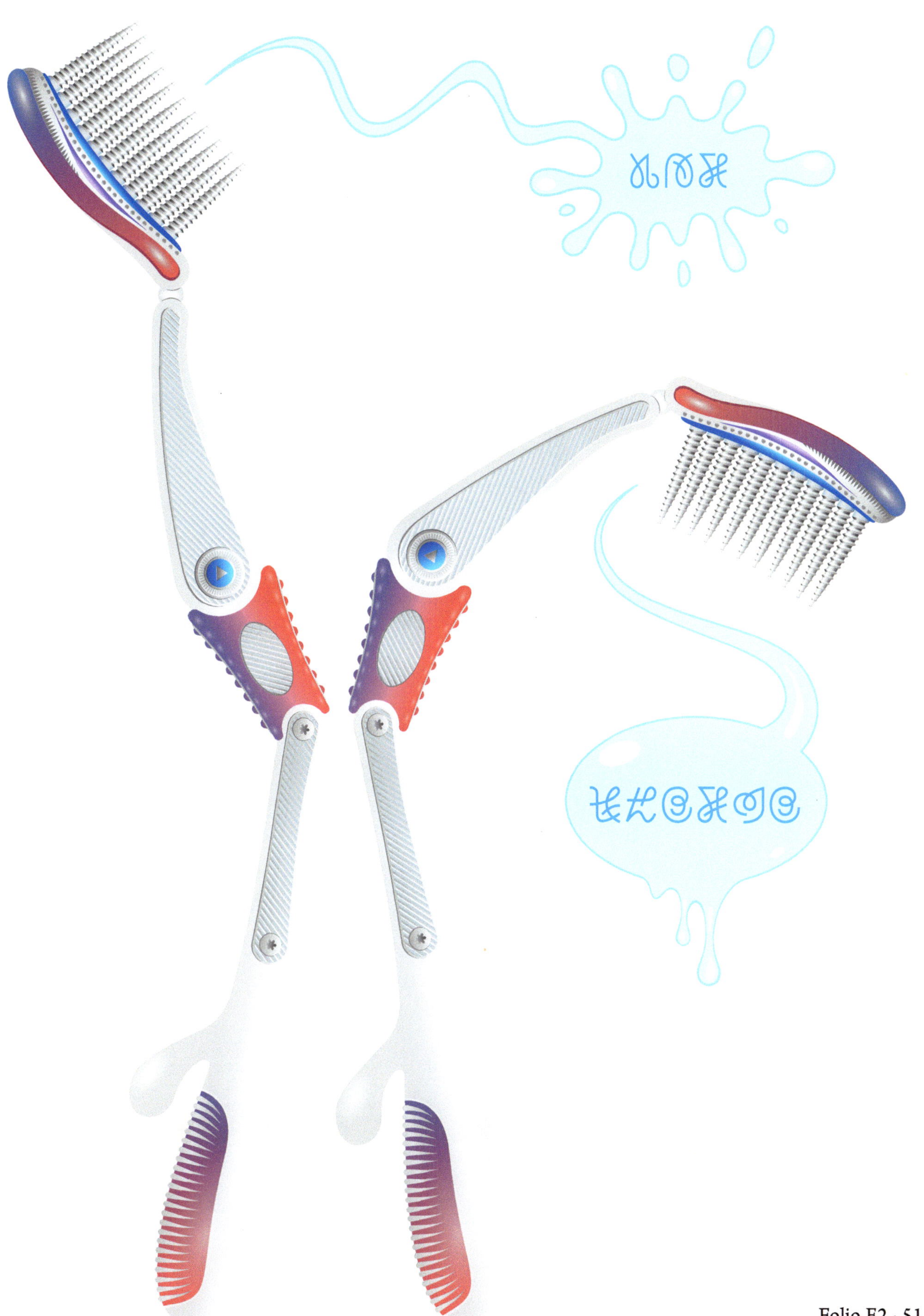

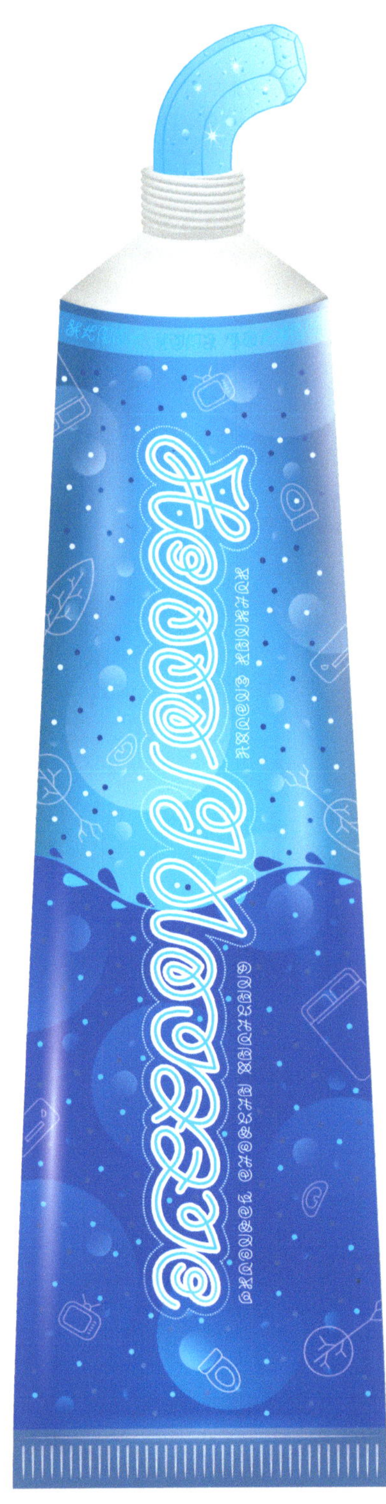

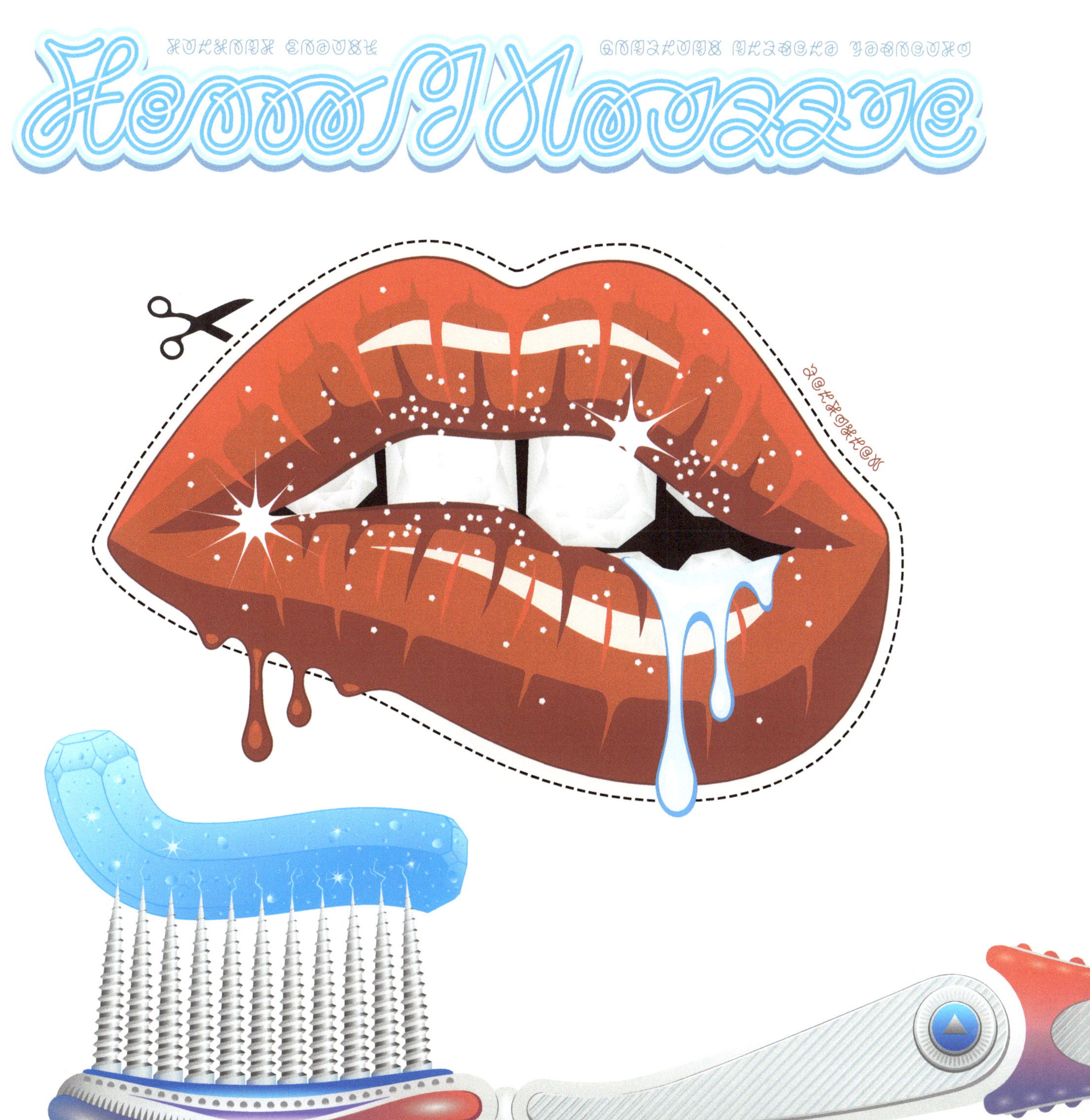

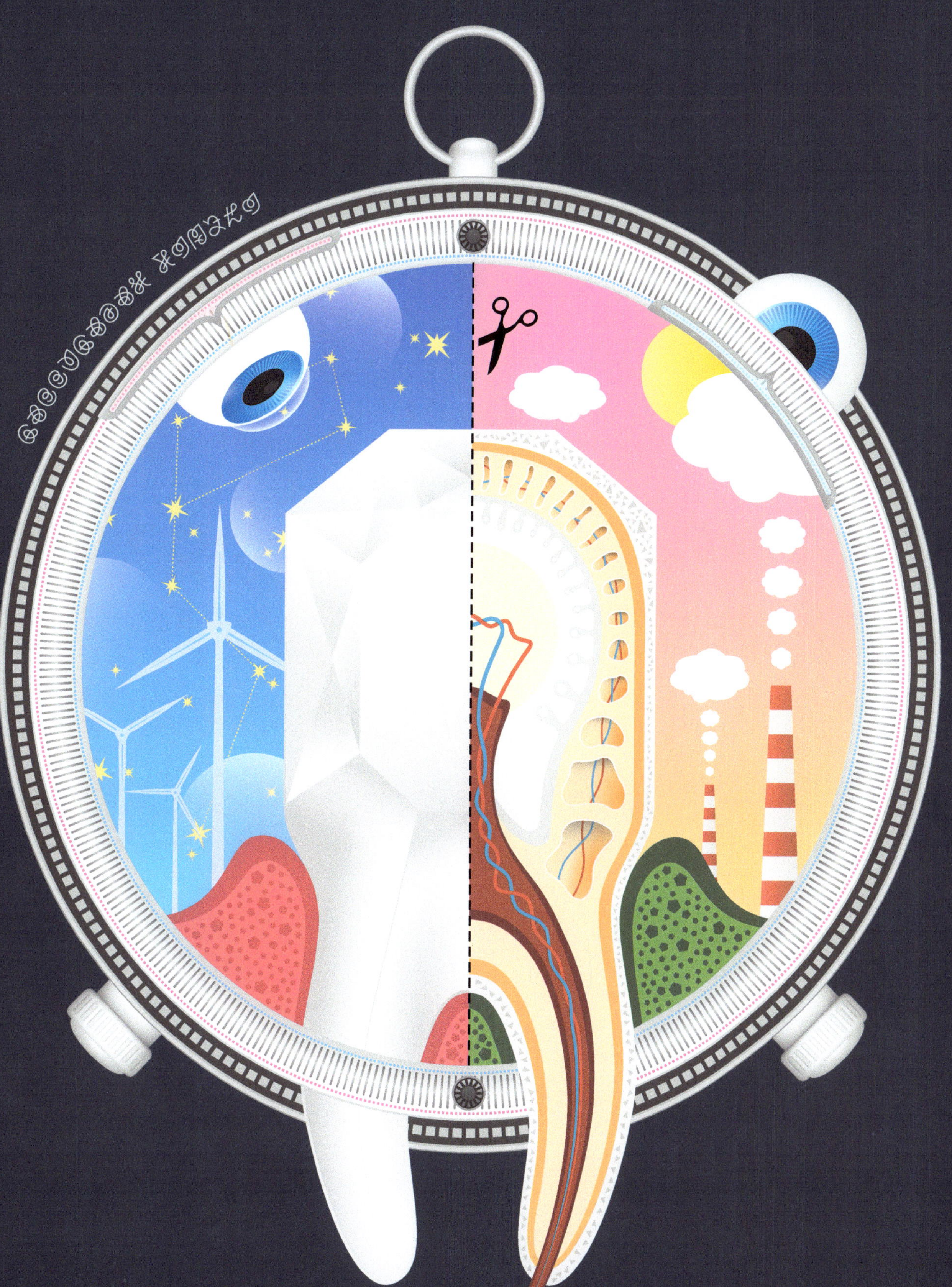

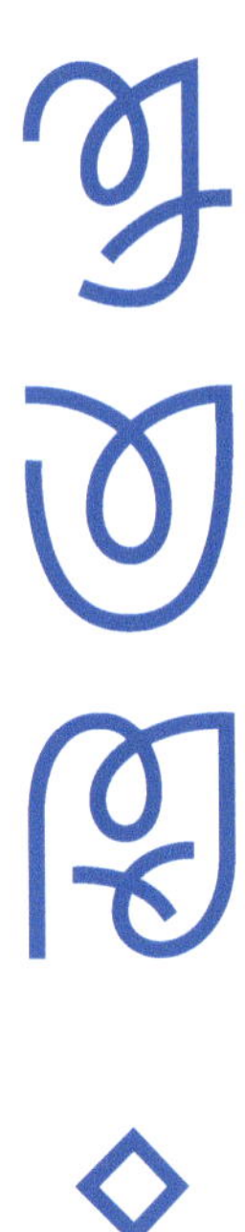